I0814387

"The poetry of George Herbert holds a hallowed place in the hearts of Christian readers who love devotional poetry. This edition of selected Herbert poems accompanied by pastoral commentary makes Herbert an even greater treasure."

Leland Ryken, Professor of English Emeritus, Wheaton College

"Herbert's poetry pulses with praise and pierces with sorrow. It wonders. It beckons. It brings us into the presence of God and deepens our spiritual lives. With a trusted guide like Stephen Witmer, the poems of George Herbert can become friends and companions along the way of life—voices of aid and reflection for all who seek to follow Christ. This book offers forty rich treasures for readers of every kind."

Abram van Engen, author, *Word Made Fresh: An Invitation to Poetry for the Church*

"I have never understood why George Herbert is not a household name among Christians. No other major literary author is so evangelical, so Christ-centered, so biblical, so devotional. Stephen Witmer briefly unpacks and applies Herbert's poetry so that today's Christians can connect with a fellow believer who can deepen and enrich their faith."

Gene Edward Veith Jr., Provost Emeritus, Patrick Henry College; author, *Reformation Spirituality: The Religion of George Herbert*

"George Herbert was a man after God's own heart. With Stephen Witmer as a reliable guide, this short anthology of Herbert's best poems offers easy entrance into a remarkable resource for spiritual formation. Through his memorable, beautiful poetry, George Herbert can become one of your soul's best mentors and truest friends."

Philip Graham Ryken, President, Wheaton College

In All Things Thee to See

In All Things Thee to See

A Devotional Guide to Selected Poems of George Herbert

George Herbert

Selections and Reflections by
Stephen Witmer

WHEATON, ILLINOIS

In All Things Thee to See: A Devotional Guide to Selected Poems of George Herbert

Published by Crossway
1300 Crescent Street
Wheaton, Illinois 60187

Cover design: Jordan Singer

First printing 2026

Printed in China

All emphases in Scripture quotations have been added by the author of the reflections.

Hardcover ISBN: 979-8-8749-0074-8
ePub ISBN: 979-8-8749-0076-2
PDF ISBN: 979-8-8749-0075-5

Library of Congress Cataloging-in-Publication Data

Names: Herbert, George, 1593-1633 author | Witmer, Stephen E., 1976- editor
Title: In all things thee to see: a devotional guide to selected poems of George Herbert / George Herbert ; edited by Stephen Witmer.
Description: Wheaton : Crossway, 2026. | Includes bibliographical references and index.
Identifiers: LCCN 2025007489 (print) | LCCN 2025007490 (ebook) | ISBN 9798874900748 cloth | ISBN 9798874900755 pdf | ISBN 9798874900762 epub
Subjects: LCSH: Herbert, George, 1593-1633—Appreciation | Christian poetry, English—Early modern, 1500-1700 | LCGFT: Religious poetry
Classification: LCC PR3507.A2 W555 2026 (print) | LCC PR3507.A2 (ebook)
LC record available at https://lccn.loc.gov/2025007489
LC ebook record available at https://lccn.loc.gov/2025007490

Crossway is a publishing ministry of Good News Publishers.

RRD 35 34 33 32 31 30 29 28 27 26
15 14 13 12 11 10 9 8 7 6 5 4 3 2 1

For my beloved Pepperell Christian Fellowship church family, with deep gratitude and great delight.

A man that looks on glass,
On it may stay his eye;
Or if he pleaseth, through it pass,
And then the heav'n espy.

GEORGE HERBERT

"The Elixir"

Contents

Introduction

WELCOME! This volume of forty George Herbert poems is for you. Perhaps you know little to nothing of Herbert and his work. If so, you're an especially honored guest. In fact, I've written with you particularly in mind. I'm eager to guide you to rich poetic and spiritual fare and enjoy it with you. Please, sit and eat. Alternatively, maybe you have savored Herbert for a long time. I'm very glad to hear it. There will be plenty in this book for you to enjoy too. Whatever your prior knowledge and experience, my prayer is that Herbert's poems will lead you to know Christ more fully and love him more deeply. That's what they've done for me, somewhat to my own surprise.

I was first drawn to Herbert for his prose rather than his poetry. I read him not because I knew him to be a great poet but because I heard he was a good pastor. While writing a book on small-town ministry, I discovered he had written his own rural ministry handbook (*The Country Parson*) four hundred years ago. Curious, I dipped into a volume of Herbert's complete works that I had carried across an ocean, then left unread on a shelf for a decade. *The Country Parson* helped me. Herbert's life story intrigued me. But it was the poems that began to change me.

They did so by introducing me to new delights and protecting me from old despair. Imagine discovering in adulthood delicious foods you've never tasted before. That's how encountering Herbert's vibrant, vital language was for me. My life got a little bit richer, my capacity for enjoyment grew a little bit bigger. In "The Glance," Herbert wrote that he felt "a sugar'd strange delight" when God first looked upon his sinful soul. I didn't know exactly what that phrase meant, but the sound of "sugar'd" and "strange" together was sweetly pleasing, and the unexpected juxtaposition of those two words was curiously intriguing. Only later would I begin to marvel at Herbert's skill in using words to evoke the very feelings they described. Initially, I simply felt delight, and expressions such as the "full-ey'd love" of God left me wanting more.

Not only did Herbert's poems expand my enjoyment of beauty, they also shepherded me through internal struggles. Prone toward sometimes crippling anxiety myself, I found in Herbert an honest, faith-filled fellow struggler. Countless Sunday mornings, I have awakened at 4 a.m., unable to fall back asleep knowing I'd soon be preaching to my congregation. I'd wrestle with despairing thoughts accusing me of not having done enough for struggling church ministries and straggling church members. Would the morning's sermon fly or flop? In such times, Herbert's poem "Aaron" became a dear companion, shepherding me toward Christ, "my alone only heart and breast." Hope would rise as I looked to him, "new drest [dressed]" in Christ's righteousness rather than my own.

Might Herbert have a similar impact on you? Could he provide fresh joy and wise care for your soul? Could he lead you to more of Christ? That's my prayer for you.

We'll begin with a brief introduction to the man and his work, an explanation of why I chose these particular poems, and some guidance on how best to engage with them.[1] Then we'll get to the poems themselves. This volume is all about the poems. My brief comments in the "Savoring the poem" sections will explain unfamiliar words and concepts while guiding you into a deeper enjoyment of the poems. Short application sections ("Shepherded by the poem") will gesture toward ways in which the poems might shape you. Think of me as the guide showing you the museum, the spotlight operator illumining the actor, or the jeweler displaying the diamond. Or, rather, don't think of me at all. Forget the jeweler and delight in the diamond.

George Herbert

George Herbert was born in 1593, during the long reign of Queen Elizabeth, who had fully instituted Protestantism in England after her father, Henry VIII, separated from the Catholic Church, creating the Church of England in 1534. It was a time of great religious earnestness and remarkable literary activity. The Act of Uniformity in 1559 had made the *Book of Common Prayer* (1559) the rule of worship throughout England. Calvinism was the dominant theology of the church. Puritans had emerged within the church, calling for it to remove Catholic ceremonies and practices, and they were willing to be imprisoned for their convictions. William Shakespeare was composing plays and John Donne was writing poems. The King James Bible would be published in 1611.

Part of a wealthy, aristocratic family, George Herbert enjoyed an outstanding education. He distinguished himself as a scholar, became a fellow at the University of Cambridge, and was appointed to the prestigious post of Orator of the University in 1620, delivering orations in Latin for significant academic occasions. That position earned him the attention of King James I, the monarch who ascended to the throne after Elizabeth I died in 1603. Herbert's star was rising. Then it wasn't. Life took some unexpected turns. The career it seemed he might enjoy in the king's court didn't materialize. Following several uncertain years living with wealthy relatives, he became an Anglican vicar in the village of Bemerton, near Salisbury. He served there in relative obscurity for three years and then died of sickness in 1633, shortly before his fortieth birthday.

And that may have been that. He might easily have been forgotten by all but academic historians. It's true that he was respected for his polished Latin orations, that he composed some Latin poems and collected many proverbs, and that he wrote *The Country Parson*. But none of those account for his impact on contemporary readers. His enduring influence rests on a slender volume of about 160 English poems (depending on how you count them) that might well never have seen the light of day.

The Temple

On Herbert's deathbed, he sent those unpublished poems to his friend Nicholas Ferrar with instructions to burn or print them, as his friend saw fit. Ferrar read them, was deeply moved, and published the volume almost immediately, calling it *The Temple*. It was an instant and massive success, going through numerous editions in its first decades and establishing Herbert as one of the most popular devotional poets of the seventeenth century. In every generation since, readers have benefited—including Richard Baxter, Charles Spurgeon, Samuel Taylor Coleridge, W. H. Auden, and T. S. Eliot. The anguished William Cowper found solace in Herbert's poems. C. S. Lewis included *The Temple* among the ten books that most influenced him.[2] The philosopher Simone Weil said that during a recitation of Herbert's poem "Love (III)," Christ himself came down and took possession of her. In our own day, the poems continue to intrigue and attract Christians and non-Christians alike. On February 17, 2014, the British newspaper *The Guardian* published an article by Miranda Threlfall-Holmes titled "George Herbert: The Man Who Converted Me from Atheism."[3]

The Temple has three sections. The first, "The Church-Porch," consisting of seventy-seven stanzas, is sometimes ingenious, amusing, and helpfully memorable, and it forms an approach to what follows in the middle section. It can be rather preachy and moralizing, and it's not the main attraction. Neither is the final section, "The Church Militant," a longish poem that deals with the history of the church and a vision of future judgment upon it. It's the middle section, "The Church," that embodies Herbert's genius and accounts for his enduring influence. These poems have connected deeply with both Christian and non-Christian readers. They're why Herbert is considered one of the greatest religious poets ever.

The Poems in This Volume

The poems included in this volume are drawn from "The Church" section and account for roughly a quarter of the poems in *The Temple*. So why these particular poems? The Nobel-prize-winning Irish poet Seamus Heaney once distinguished between poems you admire outside of yourself, like produce in the market, and poems that grow *inside* you, changing you.[4] Years ago, while reading through Herbert's poems over the course of a summer, I chose fifty I thought might grow inside me. Since then, many of them have taken root and borne good fruit, inviting me into new understandings and experiences of Christ and of myself. For this volume, I've drawn from that original list of fifty, added a few others that have captured me since, and favored shorter, accessible poems, particularly those that are theologically rich and fruitfully relevant for Christians today. I hope they'll change you from the inside out, as they have me.[5]

How to Read These Poems

How should we read Herbert's poetry? How can we most profit from his work? I've found three approaches particularly helpful.

1. Read Herbert for pleasure. Here's a simple method for starting with Herbert.

Step 1: Find a poem you enjoy. It doesn't really matter *why* you enjoy it (a fresh thought, an arresting phrase, a feeling you get), just that you do.

Step 2: Linger with that one you love. Explore and enjoy it.

Step 3: Repeat steps 1–2.

This method has the merit of reading Herbert the way Herbert himself asks to be read:

> Harken unto a Verser, who may chance
> Rhyme thee to good, and make a bait of pleasure.
> A verse may find him, who a sermon flies,
> And turn delight into a sacrifice.
>
> "The Church-Porch," stanza 1

Herbert meant these poems to please and delight us. The pleasure lures us, and the delight becomes a sacrifice of worship.

T. S. Eliot once wrote,

> With the appreciation of Herbert's poems, as with all poetry, enjoyment is the beginning as well as the end. We must enjoy the poetry before we attempt to penetrate the poet's mind; we must enjoy it before we understand it, if the attempt to understand it is to be worth the trouble.[6]

Robert Frost said that a good poem "begins in delight and ends in wisdom."[7] An authority much higher than either Eliot or Frost says,

"Great are the works of the LORD, studied by all who delight in them" (Ps. 111:2). Affection spurs inspection. So start by looking for the ones you love. Abram Van Engen offers this freeing counsel for engaging with poetry:

> Read just for the joy of it. Do not feel compelled to have deep thoughts or earth-shattering revelations. If such things come, welcome them. But mostly they won't. . . . When you run into poems you find boring or odd or off-putting, feel free to set them down and try other poems. The great glory of being a full-grown adult is that there is no test—or at least, no test about poetry. You don't have to read any poem that you'd rather not read. Skip ahead. Pick a different book. Ignore some poems and focus on others. You're in charge. No one is watching you. The only task is to find a poem that somehow reaches you—something that causes you to respond. Set aside all else.[8]

This volume contains forty Herbert poems that I love. They've wooed me with beauty, wowed me with technical mastery, surprised me with unexpected twists, and soothed me with gospel truth. I hope you'll agree with me at least once. It takes just one. It begins with pleasure. That's why the first section heading under each of the poems in this volume is called "Savoring the poem." Notice, we're not merely studying it (important as that is) but *enjoying* it. That's the place to begin. Enjoyment spurs examination, which leads, in turn, to even greater enjoyment.

2. Read Herbert for pastoral guidance. He was a parish priest. The farmers and manual laborers of Bemerton didn't walk past his manse and proudly proclaim to their friends that the famous poet lived there, because he wasn't yet a famous poet. Instead, they knew him as their pastor. He preached on Sundays, catechized them in their homes, and visited the poor of the parish. Biographers tell us he loved his congregation and was loved by them. We know from *The Country Parson* that he thought deeply about how to shepherd them.

And, importantly, his pastoral calling reached through the parish and into the poems. His poetic aim wasn't primarily self-expression, the production of great art, or the securing of fame (remember, his English poems were published in print only after his death). Rather, he sought to shepherd souls, to pastor through poetry. We've already seen in the first stanza of "The Church-Porch" that his goal for the poems was to "rhyme thee to good." In his dedication to *The Temple*, he asks God to "turn their eyes hither, who shall make a gain." Mark that. He's writing for our gain. In his deathbed letter, he said that if Nicholas Ferrar saw how his poems might "turn to the advantage of any dejected poor Soul," he could publish them. Notice, he's writing for our advantage. It's true that many of his poems are intensely personal. But, like the biblical psalmists before him, he serves and shepherds his readers by generously inviting us into his experience. He makes room for us to relate to his struggles and successes, to better understand our story through his own. As stated in "Obedience," he wants us to thrust our hearts into his lines. He's a true pastor. Herbert scholar Helen Wilcox even argues that his poems "themselves enact the functions of a priest."[9]

So where exactly is Herbert the poet-shepherd guiding his flock of readers? The ultimate answer is: to more of God. Herbert was captivated by the majesty and mercy of God. Helen Wilcox writes, "The subject of every single poem in *The Temple* is, in one way or another, God."[10] Herbert's theology and poetry were deeply God-centered and profoundly influenced by the theology of the Reformation.[11] His God was sovereign. As he says in "Providence":

We all acknowledge both thy power and love
To be exact, transcendent, and divine;

Who dost so strongly and so sweetly move,
While all things have their will, yet none but thine.

God moves strongly *and* sweetly. His will is unthwartable, and that's good news. Importantly, Herbert's embrace of Reformation theology doesn't undermine the universal nature of his appeal. Rather, as Gene Edward Veith argues, his poems convey "from the inside" the positive vision of a sovereign God and thus connect with readers of all sorts.[12] Augustine was Herbert's favorite theologian. (He owned a set of Augustine's works and bequeathed them to his curate at his death). Herbert's biographer John Drury suggests that the autobiographical nature of Augustine's *Confessions* helped to inspire Herbert's own autobiographical poetry.[13] Also like the *Confessions*, many of Herbert's poems are addressed directly to God. They're never trifling or silly, because they're prayers. He saw each poem as a gift *from* and *for* the great God he loved. In his dedicatory poem for *The Temple*, Herbert writes, "Lord, my first fruits present themselves to thee; / Yet not mine neither: for from thee they came, / And must return."

So, as you read, be pastored by a man who yearns to give you more of God. The second heading under each poem in this volume is "Shepherded by the poem." This is important. If we embrace the poems purely for pleasure (pleasure as the whole shebang, rather than a starting point) or if we engage the poems merely to analyze and understand them, then we fail to experience them as Herbert intends. He means his poems to be no mere objects for inspection, but active agents of direction, counsel, care, awakening, and adoration. Let's read them along the grain of his intention, inviting them to change us. Let's receive the shepherding care of Pastor George.

3. Read Herbert for the poetry. Most of us have certain tasks we prefer to avoid. I dislike husking corn. It takes time and effort to remove the rough green sheath around the cob, then a lot of fiddly work to strip the sticky silks. What a nuisance. I care about the sweet, tender corn on the cob—all that other stuff just gets thrown away. And this is the way many people read poetry. The "message" of the poem is the valuable part. All the rest is a bother. On this approach, once we've figured out the message, the poem has done its job, delivered the goods, and can now be discarded, like the Amazon boxes in your recycling bin. If only poets could state crisply and clearly what they meant, poetry would be so much more efficient. Think of all the time saved!

Is this a good approach to poetry? Not at all, because poetry doesn't just express ideas, it *embodies* them. A good poem engages our senses and emotions, providing rich, condensed *experiences* of the beauty, confusion, surprise, sadness, and delight we feel in life. For that reason, we never get past the poem itself—nor are we meant to. The best analogy for a poem is not a discardable husk but a human body. Think of time spent with your closest, dearest friends. You invariably encounter and enjoy them as living souls in physical bodies. Their voices, faces, distinctive movements, and bodily limitations are what make them *them* and are inseparable from your experience and enjoyment of them. The same is true for a poem. If you try to extract the "message," leaving behind the words, the shape, the meter, and the rhyme, you've lost the poem.

All of this is true especially for Herbert's poetry, because he doesn't just state truth, he offers *experiences* of it. For example, when he describes something beautiful, he does so in beautiful language. As he writes in "The Forerunners,": "Beauty and beauteous words should go together." He wants us to experience beauty in our bones, not just think it in our heads. In this volume, we'll encounter numerous instances of Herbert's poems *doing what they say*. We'll feel the brokenness of weak and sinful souls in a fallen world. We'll experience the goodness of a loving Savior. Herbert's poems hum with actuality. Reading him as a poet (not just a purveyor of truth claims) means opening ourselves to the experiences he offers.

There you have it. Read Herbert for pleasure. Welcome him as your pastor. Experience him as a poet. There's no time like the present to begin employing these three approaches. Forty transformative poems lie before you. Enjoy!

The Altar

A broken ALTAR, Lord, thy servant rears,
Made of a heart, and cemented with tears:
Whose parts are as thy hand did frame;
No workman's tool hath touch'd the same.
A HEART alone
Is such a stone,
As nothing but
Thy pow'r doth cut.
Wherefore each part
Of my hard heart
Meets in this frame,
To praise thy Name;
That, if I chance to hold my peace,
These stones to praise thee may not cease.
O let thy blessed SACRIFICE be mine,
And sanctify this ALTAR to be thine.

Savoring the poem. This poem is sheer genius. It's a figure poem, visually in the shape of what it's about, and Herbert even manages to place the "sacrifice" (in the penultimate line) on the "altar" (in the final line). Our senses are immediately engaged. We're beckoned to hear, see, and feel the poem. Remarkably, the constraints of visually shaping the words haven't resulted in stilted speech. Listen to it read aloud and you'll hear its easy, natural flow. The poem is about more than one thing. Here is a thrilling, Scripture-infused vision of what it means to be a new covenant believer. Jesus has died for his people. Broken, repentant hearts have been transformed by God (in order to unlock the biblical background, see Deut. 27:2–6; Ps. 51:17; Ezek. 11:19; Luke 19:40; 2 Cor. 3:3). And as the reciprocity of the final two lines makes clear, God is now ours and we are his. Here also is a statement about Herbert's *poetry*, the goal of which is whole-hearted, enduring praise of God's name within the "frame" of his poems. Standing at the beginning of "The Church" section (the main body of poems in *The Temple*), "The Altar" establishes the aim of all that follows.

Shepherded by the poem. God's power cuts the hard stone of our hearts, fashioning us into forgiven, transformed worshipers. Notice a paradox: while Herbert speaks in the first line of "a broken Altar," his visualized altar form is intact. Herbert loved wordplay and frequently used titles with double meanings. Here, he may be punning on God's ability to *alter* or adjust a broken heart by fashioning it, through affliction and tears, into a place of praise. How has God worked through suffering and weeping in your own life? How has he altered your hard heart, making it an altar of worship?

The Agony

Philosophers have measur'd mountains,
Fathom'd the depths of seas, of states, and kings,
Walk'd with a staff to heav'n, and traced fountains:
But there are two vast, spacious things,
The which to measure it doth more behove:
Yet few there are that sound them; Sin and Love.

Who would know Sin, let him repair
Unto mount Olivet; there shall he see
A man so wrung with pains, that all his hair,
His skin, his garments bloody be.
Sin is that press and vice, which forceth pain
To hunt his cruel food through ev'ry vein.

Who knows not Love, let him assay
And taste that juice, which on the cross a pike
Did set again abroach; then let him say
If ever he did taste the like.
Love is that liquor sweet and most divine,
Which my God feels as blood; but I, as wine.

Philosophers: learned individuals, scientists. **Behove:** archaic form of "behoove," meaning "to be advantageous." **Sound:** plumb the depths of. **Repair:** go. **Assay:** attempt. **Pike:** spear. **Abroach:** having let out a liquid.

Savoring the poem. Consider the vast field of human intellectual pursuit, from ocean depths to mountain heights, from quarks to koalas. Staggeringly impressive, but, according to Herbert, we're missing something. It's *most* important to understand sin and love, though not many make those subjects their expertise. If you'd like to try (and Herbert hopes you will), two things will help: a Bible and Holy Communion. Both focus your senses on Jesus's passion (his agony), and his passion will show you sin and love. Read the gospel accounts of Jesus in the garden of Gethsemane (Matt. 26:36–46; Mark 14:32–42; Luke 22:39–46; John 18:1–11) and *see* in your mind's eye his sweaty, bloody struggle. Sin did that. It shot pain through every vein. *How wicked is sin?* Come to the Communion table during gathered worship. *Taste* the wine. Drink down the love of the Savior who bled for you. *How wonderful is love!* Our sin makes God's love supremely painful for him (he feels it as the spilled blood of judgment) and supremely pleasant for us (we drink it as the sweet wine of fellowship).

Shepherded by the poem. Herbert was a local priest who loved his congregation. In this poem, Pastor George shepherds our souls by inviting us to explore sin and love simultaneously. That's because he knows it's fruitless—and dangerous—to pursue knowledge of one without the other. Plumbing our sin apart from God's love drags us down to despair; praising God's love apart from our sin leaves us in the shallows. When we know God's love, we have courage to acknowledge our sin. When we face our sin, we thrill to the wonder of God's love. So Herbert focuses our imaginations and taste buds on Jesus's passion, which reveals both sin and love. As Tim Keller (a fan of Herbert) has famously said, "The gospel is this: We are more sinful and flawed in ourselves than we ever dared believe, yet at the very same time we are more loved and accepted in Jesus Christ than we ever dared hope."[14] How might this poem shape your next experience at the Communion table? How might it affect your relationship with God every day of your life?

Redemption

Having been tenant long to a rich Lord,
	Not thriving, I resolved to be bold,
	And make a suit unto him, to afford
A new small-rented lease, and cancel th' old.

In heaven at his manor I him sought:
	They told me there, that he was lately gone
	About some land, which he had dearly bought
Long since on earth, to take possession.

I straight return'd, and knowing his great birth,
	Sought him accordingly in great resorts;
	In cities, theaters, gardens, parks, and courts:
At length I heard a ragged noise and mirth

	Of thieves and murderers: there I him espied,
	Who straight, *Your suit is granted,* said, & died.

Suit: petition. **Lately:** recently. **Straight:** immediately

Savoring the poem. The key to this allegorical sonnet is the terminology of "new" and "old" in the fourth line. It's about the need for the old covenant to be renegotiated (one meaning of the title "Redemption") and canceled with the coming of the new covenant (Heb. 8:13). Of course, Herbert could have written about this in prose—he was, after all, a learned pastor-scholar. Instead, he writes a narrative poem. Why? Because he wants to do more than convey theological truth. He wants us to *feel* the surprise of how God achieves his redemptive plan. Read this story as though it's new to you, as though you've missed Herbert's wink with the word "heaven" in line 5 and don't know who "the rich Lord" is. Now feel the two-word electric jolt of the poem's ending: "& died." What a shocking final line. The suit is granted. *Yes!* The rich Lord dies. *What?* But this is the Christian story. In fact, the Christian story is more surprising still. Redemption and new covenant blessing are won through that death—not in the resorts of the high-born, but amidst riff-raff with ragged noise on a cross.

Shepherded by the poem. The word "straight" in the final line repays our reflection. To this point in the story, the speaker's efforts have been featured extensively. He has traveled far and searched carefully for his Lord, all for the purpose of renegotiating their contract. Now, finally, he sees the Lord. Will he need to argue him into new terms? Will the negotiations be arduous? Not at all. No argument, no negotiation—apparently, not even a *request*. Jesus came for this purpose, and his "straight" response conveys his eagerness to die for his own, securing a new covenant for them (Heb. 8:8–12). This is the loving heart of Christ for you.

Easter wings

Lord, who createdst man in wealth and store,
Though foolishly he lost the same,
Decaying more and more,
Till he became
Most poor:
With thee
Oh let me rise
As larks, harmoniously,
And sing this day thy victories:
Then shall the fall further the flight in me.

My tender age in sorrow did begin:
  And still with sicknesses and shame
    Thou didst so punish sin,
      That I became
        Most thin.
        With thee
      Let me combine
    And feel this day thy victory:
  For, if I imp my wing on thine
Affliction shall advance the flight in me.

Imp: to graft feathers into a bird's wing to improve its flight

Savoring the poem. Here is another figure poem (like "The Altar") meant to engage our ears and eyes, and by which Herbert will *show* us something rather than merely telling us. Not only will he write words about wings; he will arrange those words in the shape of wings. Notice that the fullness of the first line of stanza 1 visually expresses what it says ("Lord, who createdst man in wealth and store"). Then lines 2–5 grow progressively shorter. Line 5 is just two thin words. Through line length, we're viewing the devastating effects of the fall, which stripped humankind of the "wealth and store" that God provided in a perfect creation (Genesis 1–2). Worse, humankind has lost fellowship with God himself (note that God, mentioned in the first line, is absent from the following four). We're all prodigal sons and line 5 is the pigsty.

But that's not the end of the story, because there's good news in line 6: "With thee." "Thee" is Christ, the turning point of the first stanza, who meets us in our spiritual poverty by dying in our place. "While we were still sinners, Christ died for us" (Rom. 5:8). Beginning in line 7, the lines increase in amplitude, representing the blessings of Christ, through whose poverty we become rich (2 Cor. 8:9). Because he died our death, we rise with his resurrection. And stunningly, God brings about a greater good through humanity's rebellion: a repentant sinner who clings to a crucified and resurrected Christ knows the love of God more deeply than Adam did. The fall furthers flight. The end is better than the beginning. The new creation surpasses Eden.

Shepherded by the poem. In stanza 2, Herbert tells the story again, now in a more personal mode. The great narrative of humanity's sin and

Christ's provision becomes his own. Can we, like Herbert, tell both stories—one the size of the universe and the other the size of our lives? Let's study the shape of those wings carefully in order to remind ourselves of the scrawniness of a Christless life and the plentitude of a Christ-filled one. He became "most poor" and "most thin" so we could fly with him. How about enjoying flight time today? Through faith, graft his triumphant, sin-conquering wing-feathers into your sin-damaged ones. Yes, it's true we'll rise and fly on that great future day (notice the forward-looking "shall" in the final line of each stanza). But for believers, resurrection begins now, on Easter day and every day (notice "this day" in both stanzas). As we trust Christ for forgiveness and provision, let's sing his victories.

Sin (1)

Lord, with what care hast thou begirt us round!
    Parents first season us: then schoolmasters
    Deliver us to laws; they send us bound
To rules of reason, holy messengers,

Pulpits and Sundays, sorrow dogging sin,
    Afflictions sorted, anguish of all sizes,
    Fine nets and stratagems to catch us in,
Bibles laid open, millions of surprises,

Blessings beforehand, ties of gratefulness,
    The sound of glory ringing in our ears:
    Without, our shame; within, our consciences;
Angels and grace, eternal hopes and fears.

    Yet all these fences and their whole array
    One cunning bosom-sin blows quite away.

Begirt: to encircle. **Season:** to mature, strengthen. **Dogging:** following closely and persistently. **Fences:** means of security, protection, defense. **Quite:** completely

Savoring the poem. Allow yourself to bask in the loving protection of God described in the first twelve lines of this poem. Savor God's care for you. He guards and guides you in a thousand ways. He loves his children. But now feel the stunning blow of sin's lethal haymaker in the final line. It hits us out of nowhere, blindsiding us, dropping us to the mat, just when we thought we were safe. Haven't we all experienced exactly that in the course of our lives? Haven't we been taken down by a sin we didn't expect? Of course, Herbert could simply state this reality as a proposition: sin is powerful and devious, and it surprises us. But this poem is far better. It gives us an *experience* of what it says.

Shepherded by the poem. If you're looking for a quick and easy solution to sin's cunning attacks, you won't find it in this poem. Herbert is too deep a thinker and too good a pastor. This poem is a bucket of cold water, awakening us to danger. Evidently, we're meant to ponder our response. What will we do, how will we live? One good place to start is by asking, *What are my "bosom-sins"? Which temptations speak deeply to my heart? Which ones might take me out?* God graciously builds fences to protect us from sin. We should thank him for them. But the shock this poem generates at sin's power is meant to relocate our trust from the fences to the God who gives them. Let's redouble our prayers for protection and our reliance on him. Let's pray, as Jesus taught, "Lead us not into temptation, but deliver us from evil" (Matt. 6:13).

Affliction (1)

When first thou didst entice to thee my heart,
I thought the service brave:
So many joys I writ down for my part,
Besides what I might have
Out of my stock of natural delights,
Augmented with thy gracious benefits.

I looked on thy furniture so fine,
And made it fine to me:
Thy glorious household-stuff did me entwine,
And 'tice me unto thee.
Such stars I counted mine: both heav'n and earth
Paid me my wages in a world of mirth.

What pleasures could I want, whose King I served,
Where joys my fellows were?
Thus argu'd into hopes, my thoughts reserved
No place for grief or fear.
Therefore my sudden soul caught at the place,
And made her youth and fierceness seek thy face.

Brave: splendid. **Furniture . . . household-stuff:** the physical implements of the temple or the church, used here metaphorically to describe the spiritual benefits of the church. **'Tice:** entice (Herbert emphasizes his attraction to God and the church after his conversion.). **Caught at the place:** eagerly tried to lay hold of it.

AFFLICTION (I)

At first thou gav'st me milk and sweetnesses;
I had my wish and way:
My days were straw'd with flow'rs and happiness;
There was no month but May.
But with my years sorrow did twist and grow,
And made a party unawares for woe.

My flesh began unto my soul in pain,
Sicknesses cleave my bones;
Consuming agues dwell in ev'ry vein,
And tune my breath to groans.
Sorrow was all my soul; I scarce believed,
Till grief did tell me roundly, that I lived.

When I got health, thou took'st away my life,
And more; for my friends die:
My mirth and edge was lost; a blunted knife
Was of more use than I.
Thus thin and lean without a fence or friend,
I was blown through with ev'ry storm and wind.

Whereas my birth and spirit rather took
The way that takes the town;
Thou didst betray me to a lingring book,
And wrap me in a gown.
I was entangled in the world of strife,
Before I had the power to change my life.

Made a party unawares for woe: the meaning of this line isn't entirely clear; it may indicate that he was unknowingly opening himself to suffering. **Agues:** fevers. **The way that takes the town:** the path to a secular career at the king's court.

Yet, for I threatened oft the siege to raise,
Not simpring all mine age,
Thou often didst with Academic praise
Melt and dissolve my rage.
I took thy sweetened pill, till I came where
I could not go away, nor persevere.

Yet lest perchance I should too happy be
In my unhappiness,
Turning my purge to food, thou throwest me
Into more sicknesses.
Thus doth thy power cross-bias me, not making
Thine own gift good, yet me from my ways taking.

Now I am here, what thou wilt do with me
None of my books will show:
I read, and sigh, and wish I were a tree;
For sure then I should grow
To fruit or shade: at least some bird would trust
Her household to me, and I should be just.

Yet, though thou troublest me, I must be meek;
In weakness must be stout.
Well, I will change the service, and go seek
Some other master out.
Ah my dear God! though I am clean forgot,
Let me not love thee, if I love thee not.

Simpring: smirking. **Turning my purge to food:** his suffering was what he lived on. **Cross-bias:** compel a change of direction. **Stout:** strong, bravely persevering. **Clean:** completely, entirely.

Savoring the poem. A typical evangelical Christian testimony begins with the bad (without Christ) and pivots to the good (with Christ). That's not Herbert's story in "Affliction (1)," his most autobiographical poem, spoken (in good Augustinian fashion) directly and entirely to God. It all began well enough (lines 1–22), but he didn't get what he was bargaining for. Instead, he encountered severe physical illness, followed by the deaths of family members and friends, then ambivalence toward academic life, and more physical affliction (lines 23–54). And it's not as though he has put all this behind him. His ignorance of the future and deep feelings of uselessness, combined with the pressure to submit to God's will, encourage present rebellious thoughts (lines 55–64). That leads to the final two lines. What do they mean? Does he feel completely forgotten by God? Does he long, nonetheless, to remain whole-heartedly devoted to God? Perhaps. It's not entirely clear! Maybe the ambiguity of these last lines expresses the uncertainty he feels,[15] just as the ambiguity of the earlier line, "And made a party unawares for woe," may express Herbert's confusion as things begin to go pear-shaped and he doubts.[16] Here's the one thing that's clear: in the face of a disappointing past, a present struggle, and an unresolved future, he loves God ("Ah my dear God!"). That's his testimony.

Shepherded by the poem. This raw outpouring stands in the tradition of biblical complaint (e.g. Psalms 22, 38, 102). When you tell your story to God, how honest are you willing to be about your disappointments and griefs? Notice a hint in line 53 that God is working for Herbert's good even in disappointment. Herbert says that God "cross-biased" him. Though he means that God stymied and redirected him, the pun on "cross" points to God's redemptive purpose. Are you able to glimpse God's kindness even in the disappointing turns of your story? Recall and celebrate one or two such times in your life. Be as specific as you can. How about identifying a Jesus-loving friend with whom you can swap some of these faith-strengthening stories today?

Repentance

Lord, I confess my sin is great;
Great is my sin. Oh! gently treat
With thy quick flow'r, thy momentary bloom;
Whose life still pressing
Is one undressing,
A steady aiming at a tomb.

Man's age is two hours work, or three:
Each day doth round about us see.
Thus are we to delights: but we are all
To sorrows old,
If like be told
From what life feeleth, Adam's fall.

O let thy height of mercy then
Compassionate short-breathed men.
Cut me not off for my most foul transgression:
I do confess
My foolishness;
My God, accept of my confession.

Treat: deal with. **Undressing:** decaying, declining. **Compassionate:** have compassion on.

Sweeten at length this bitter bowl,
Which thou hast pour'd into my soul;
Thy wormwood turn to health, winds to fair weather:
For if thou stay,
I and this day,
As we did rise, we die together.

When thou for sin rebukest man,
Forthwith he waxeth woe and wan:
Bitterness fills our bowels; all our hearts
Pine, and decay,
And drop away,
And carry with them th' other parts.

But thou wilt sin and grief destroy;
That so the broken bones may joy,
And tune together in a well-set song,
Full of his praises,
Who dead men raises.
Fractures well cur'd make us more strong.

Savoring the poem. As the title implies, this poem is humbler and more penitent than the turbulent complaint of "Affliction (1)." Herbert tells his own story ("I" and "my" in the first line), which is simultaneously

Stay: delay, stay away. **Forthwith he waxeth wo and wan:** under God's rebuke, sinners become sorrowful and weak.

the story of God's people ("us" in the final line). It's a story of sin and suffering. Freely confessing his sin and acknowledging his fragility, Herbert pleads for God's mercy. Though he reports no divine response, his gaze fixes on the future, when God will destroy sin and grief and raise the dead. Here hope rises because Herbert sees that the brokenness he experiences now will lead to greater praise then. The final line of the poem is Herbert at his best—employing a homely truth to make a profound theological and pastoral point. A broken bone heals stronger, and a world with man's sin and Christ's grace is better than a world with neither. To borrow phrasing from "Easter wings," the fall furthers the flight.

Shepherded by the poem. The striking difference in tone between "Affliction (1)" and "Repentance" mirrors the variety of biblical psalms and gives us permission to honestly express our feelings to God in a range of ways. Notice that, in this poem, the basis of Herbert's request for forgiveness is God's great mercy and Herbert's great sin, weakness, foolishness and transitory existence. Of these, God's mercy is the greater. "O let thy height of mercy then / Compassionate short-breathed men." What areas of our lives require repentance? Here is an opportunity to bring them into the light, casting ourselves upon that towering "height of mercy." God's grace can overwhelm our sin and bring us into a brighter, gladder, sweeter season of life. Let's follow Herbert in hopeful confession. Lord, please "sweeten at length this bitter bowl."

Faith

Lord, how couldst thou so much appease
Thy wrath for sin as, when man's sight was dim,
And could see little, to regard his ease,
And bring by Faith all things to him?

Hungry I was, and had no meat:
I did conceit a most delicious feast;
I had it straight, and did as truly eat,
As ever did a welcome guest.

There is a rare outlandish root,
Which when I could not get, I thought it here:
That apprehension cur'd so well my foot,
That I can walk to heav'n well near.

I owed thousands and much more:
I did believe that I did nothing owe,
And liv'd accordingly; my creditor
Believes so too, and lets me go.

Faith makes me any thing, or all
That I believe is in the sacred story:
And where sin placeth me in Adam's fall,
Faith sets me higher in his glory.

Conceit: imagine, conceive. **Straight:** immediately. **Outlandish:** foreign. **Root:** a medicinal plant.

If I go lower in the book,
What can be lower than the common manger?
Faith puts me there with him, who sweetly took
Our flesh and frailty, death and danger.

If bliss had lien in art or strength,
None but the wise or strong had gained it:
Where now by Faith all arms are of a length;
One size doth all conditions fit.

A peasant may believe as much
As a great Clerk, and reach the highest stature.
Thus dost thou make proud knowledge bend & crouch,
While grace fills up uneven nature.

When creatures had no real light
Inherent in them, thou didst make the sun
Impute a luster, and allow them bright;
And in this show, what Christ hath done.

That which before was darkned clean
With bushy groves, pricking the looker's eye,
Vanisht away, when Faith did change the scene:
And then appear'd a glorious sky.

What though my body run to dust?
Faith cleaves unto it, counting evr'y grain
With an exact and most particular trust,
Reserving all for flesh again.

Lien: an obsolete form of the word "lie," meaning "lain," that is, "if bliss had lain in art or strength." **Clerk:** clergyman. **Impute a luster:** give light to. **Clean:** completely.

Savoring the poem. Far too often, old truths turn stale. All the wonder leaks out. So we need fresh ways of seeing and saying that re-colorize the picture and reawaken awe. Poetry does that. Imagination does it too. In this poem, Herbert uses both to celebrate the ludicrous, hilarious (this poem is funny) miracle of faith. Imagine that by simply thinking of food, you had a feast before you. Imagine that by simply conceiving a cure, you were healed. Or that by believing your debt was forgiven, it was! It sounds like a fairy tale, but that's what faith does. "And to the one who does not work but believes in him who justifies the ungodly, his faith is counted as righteousness" (Rom. 4:5). This is the glorious Reformation doctrine of the imputed righteousness of Christ. (It's no accident that Herbert uses the word "impute" in line 35 to describe what the "sun" does.) Faith rewrites the biblical story, excusing us from the dead-end role of Adam (where sin had us) and exalting us (the peasant no less than the clergyman) with the glorious Christ. If you look closely, you'll see Christ throughout this poem. He's the "most delicious feast" enjoyed at the Communion table, the "root" (Isa. 11:10; 53:2; Rom. 15:12; Rev. 5:5; 22:16) who heals serpent-bruised heels (Gen. 3:15), and the creditor who releases debtors from the crushing weight of what they owe. And all this comes to us by faith. Most miraculously of all, faith guarantees life beyond this life, tracking (accountant-like) every grain of our flesh, ensuring we'll be raised whole-bodied to enjoy God forever. What a wonder!

Shepherded by the poem. The most immediate application of this poem is: believe God. Trust Christ. Herbert is gunning for our faith. But notice he never says that. Rather than commanding belief he celebrates it. This poem sparkles and inspires. Herbert blows the dust from dusty doctrine, flooding us with wonder at the miracle of faith. That's because he's a skillful pastor. He knows we often respond better to inspiration than exhortation. He's gently guiding us to deeper trust. In which areas of your life is it currently hardest for you to trust God? His call upon us is to believe (Mark 11:24), and his gift to us is the very faith he requires (Phil. 1:29). We can learn a lot from Herbert's approach in this poem. Do some Christian truths taste as stale as the crackers in the back of your cupboard? May it never be! We're not George Herbert, but how might we exercise our sanctified imaginations in order to renew our wonder and inspire it in others? Pick a doctrine and have a go. If it doesn't make you sing, you haven't understood it yet.

Prayer (1)

Prayer the Church's banquet, Angels' age,
    God's breath in man returning to his birth,
    The soul in paraphrase, heart in pilgrimage,
The Christian plummet sounding heav'n and earth;

Engine against th' Almighty, sinners' tower,
    Reversed thunder, Christ-side-piercing spear,
    The six-day's world transposing in an hour,
A kind of tune, which all things hear and fear;

Softness, and peace, and joy, and love, and bliss,
    Exalted Manna, gladness of the best,
    Heaven in ordinary, man well dressed,
The Milky Way, the bird of Paradise,

    Church-bells beyond the stars heard, the soul's blood,
    The land of spices; something understood.

Angels' age: limitless. **Plummet:** an instrument for measuring the depth of water. **Engine:** an instrument of warfare. **The land of spices:** a meeting place between Christ and the human soul, with overtones of Eden and the garden in Song of Solomon 4:12–16.[17]

Savoring the poem. The most striking feature of this sonnet is what it's missing. There's not a single verb in the entire thing. Instead, Herbert provides a stunning flow of twenty-seven rapid-fire descriptions of prayer, ranging from gentle, reassuring images to violent, martial ones. Prayer is endlessly varied and interesting. It's nourishing and celebratory ("the Church's banquet"). It involves sweet reciprocity with God ("God's breath in man returning to his birth") and bellicose complaint against him ("Engine against th' Almighty"). Prayer is not one thing but many. This is clearly a poem by a praying man who has conversed with God at lots of times in lots of ways. We have much to learn from him.

Shepherded by the poem. Don't worry if you don't understand every image for prayer in this poem. After all, the final description, "something understood," is not exactly crystal clear! Part of the genius of poetry is its ambiguity, which reflects the ambiguities of life—and of prayer, for that matter. Sometimes, prayer raises more questions than it answers. Rather than fretting over these images, linger with them. Consider pondering one a day for a month. (I did, and it was very good for my soul.) When it comes to meditating on and applying the insights of this poem, Herbert's corporate focus is particularly important. Private, personal prayer is a wonderful thing, but here Herbert seems to be thinking mainly of prayer as a source of nourishment and refreshment for God's gathered people—his first image is "the Church's banquet." How can you savor the feast together with your own local church family? Are there regular rhythms of gathered prayer that you can join? If one doesn't currently exist within your church family, how about starting it?

The Temper (1)

How should I praise thee, Lord! how should my rhymes
Gladly engrave thy love in steel,
If what my soul doth feel sometimes,
My soul might ever feel!

Although there were some forty heav'ns, or more,
Sometimes I peer above them all;
Sometimes I hardly reach a score,
Sometimes to hell I fall.

O rack me not to such a vast extent;
Those distances belong to thee:
The world's too little for thy tent,
A grave too big for me.

Wilt thou meet arms with man, that thou dost stretch
A crumb of dust from heav'n to hell?
Will great God measure with a wretch?
Shall he thy stature spell?

Temper: temperament, frame of mind. **Rack:** To be stretched out on a rack (an instrument of torture). **Meet arms:** take up armaments against. A pun is possible here; there could also be allusion to Christ's outstretched, crucified arms touching those of humanity.

O let me, when thy roof my soul hath hid,
O let me roost and nestle there:
Then of a sinner thou art rid,
And I of hope and fear.

Yet take thy way; for sure thy way is best:
Stretch or contract me, thy poor debtor:
This is but tuning of my breast,
To make the music better.

Whether I fly with angels, fall with dust,
Thy hands made both, and I am there:
Thy power and love, my love and trust
Make one place ev'ry where.

Savoring the poem. George Herbert was a virtuoso, a talent for the ages, an extraordinary artist—and an ordinary human being. He felt what we often do and expressed it better than we ever can. That's why his work still resonates and elevates readers. In this poem, he wrestles with a common Christian problem: his experience of God fluctuates wildly. Sometimes he's up (*really* up, above the highest heaven) and sometimes he's down (hell-level down). He holds God responsible, imagining himself on the rack and God as the torturer. The extremes of his experience stretch him to agony. He argues and pleads for the pain to stop.

When thy roof my soul hath hid: a reference to heaven, where Herbert longs to dwell.

It doesn't work. But though his spiritual experience remains unsteady, his acceptance of God's ways stabilizes ("yet" in line 21). He sees that the fluctuation of his experience (his "temper") is in fact God's tuning ("tempering") of him like a musical instrument and forging ("tempering") of him like steel. God is making his life sweeter and stronger. This divinely powerful love calls forth Herbert's love, and finally his trust. He knows that whether he flies or falls, God is there with him.

Shepherded by the poem. When have you felt closest to God? When has he seemed most distant? In what ways can you identify with Herbert's struggle? How would you express your own experience? How might this poem help you? Often, we don't enjoy our present circumstances—they may even feel torturous. But can we, like Herbert, struggle through to the "yet take thy way" of line 21, a turn which itself echoes Jesus's "Thy will be done" (Matt. 26:42 KJV) in the garden of Gethsemane? Loving and trusting God in our present situation tunes our lives for his glory. And it ensures his presence with us—whether in the heights or depths.

The Holy Scriptures (1)

Oh Book! infinite sweetness! let my heart
        Suck ev'ry letter, and a honey gain,
        Precious for any grief in any part;
To clear the breast, to mollify all pain.

Thou art all health, health thriving till it make
        A full eternity: thou art a mass
        Of strange delights, where we may wish & take.
Ladies, look here; this is the thankful glass,

That mends the looker's eyes: this is the well
        That washes what it shows. Who can endear
        Thy praise too much? thou art heav'ns Lidger here,
Working against the states of death and hell.

        Thou art joy's handsel: heav'n lies flat in thee,
        Subject to ev'ry mounter's bended knee.

Mollify: to soften, reduce the severity of. **Endear:** place stress upon, emphasize. **Lidger:** ambassador; additionally, "lidger" is a variant (now obsolete) of "ledger," a book for keeping accounts. The pun on "ledger" expresses the Reformation conviction that the written book of Scripture is God's ambassador to the world. **Handsel:** first installment.

Savoring the poem. Herbert is adept at treating lofty topics using the imagery of everyday life, a skill he surely honed as the pastor of a tiny, rural church. In this poem, he writes of Holy Scripture—or, rather, he writes *to* Holy Scripture, addressing it directly throughout. His imaginative descriptions burst forth, Psalm 119-like, one after the other. Scripture is honey—sweet and medicinally useful. It's an abundance of delights that stoke and satisfy desire ("where we may wish & take"). It's a mirror that improves your sight. It's a well that reflects *and washes* your face. It's an ambassador of heaven, countering God's enemies. It's the first installment of heavenly joy. It makes God accessible to all who approach in repentance and prayer (note the playful paradox of mounting to heaven by bending the knee). Herbert pulls out all the stops in this poem, even assuming the persona of a man hawking mirrors to ladies in the marketplace (lines 8–9)!

Shepherded by the poem. Does the Bible taste like honey to you, or like mere paper and ink? Does it heal your body and soul or just teach you facts? Does it create and quench spiritual thirst? Does it wash and cleanse? Does it spur a hankering for heaven? It's clear from Herbert's many Scripture-permeated poems that he was a master of Bible knowledge. But before he comes to laud close study of the Bible (as he'll do in "The Holy Scriptures (2)"), he first celebrates the beauty, sweetness, and delight of God's word. He knows that we study most closely whatever delights us most deeply (Ps. 111:2). If you're not feeling desire for Scripture, and you'd like to, recognize that it's a divine gift. The Lord opened Lydia's heart to pay attention to the words of the apostle Paul (Acts 16:14), and we need the same intervention. Let's ask God for it. "Incline my heart to your testimonies, and not to selfish gain!" (Ps. 119:36). It's a prayer he delights to answer.

Grace

My stock lies dead, and no increase
Doth my dull husbandry improve:
O let thy graces without cease
Drop from above!

If still the sun should hide his face,
Thy house would but a dungeon prove,
Thy works night's captives: O let grace
Drop from above!

The dew doth ev'ry morning fall;
And shall the dew out-strip thy Dove?
The dew, for which grass cannot call,
Drop from above.

Death is still working like a mole,
And digs my grave at each remove:
Let grace work too, and on my soul
Drop from above.

Stock: a tree trunk without branches; animals on a farm. **Husbandry:** management of plants or animals.

Sin is still hammering my heart
Unto a hardness, void of love:
Let suppling grace, to cross his art,
Drop from above.

O come! for thou dost know the way:
Or if to me thou wilt not move,
Remove me, where I need not say,
Drop from above.

Savoring the poem. Until we feel helpless, we won't plead for divine help. In this poem, Herbert does both. On his own, he has failed to steward his gifting for the good of the world. On his own, no one would witness his good works even if he managed to do a few. On his own, death will get him in the end. On his own, sin will harden and isolate him. This poem is the cry of a man who has given up on himself. That's why he's looking up, not in. Grace must *drop*. But the thing is, Herbert doesn't see any help coming from above. This confuses and upsets him. The unasked-for dew refreshes the Bemerton grass each morning, but the Holy Spirit for whom he longs hasn't shown. That seems all wrong. Some poems (perhaps most famously, John Newton's hymn "Amazing Grace") savor and celebrate God's help. This is not one of those poems. It doesn't praise God for what he has given; instead, it asks God for what he *hasn't* yet given. The final stanza is Herbert's last, desperate

Suppling: that which makes more flexible.

gambit: God, if you're not willing to drop grace on me, take me where I no longer need to ask you to do so. The poem ends there, dangling. What will God say? We don't know. Doesn't that lack of resolution feel true to what we've all experienced at one time or another?

Shepherded by the poem. What are your current struggles and heartaches? What conversations are you having with God? What are you asking him to do for you? Perhaps you're burdened by past mistakes and failings or by the steady approach of old age, sickness, and death, or by the hardening of sin. Don't give up. Instead, look up to God for grace. The help you need isn't limited by your abilities or circumstances. It's as limitless as the God who gives it.

Matins

I cannot ope mine eyes,
But thou art ready there to catch
My morning-soul and sacrifice:
Then we must needs for that day make a match.

My God, what is a heart?
Silver, or gold, or precious stone,
Or star, or rainbow, or a part
Of all these things, or all of them in one?

My God, what is a heart?
That thou shouldst it so eye, and woo,
Pouring upon it all thy art,
As if that thou hadst nothing else to do?

Indeed man's whole estate
Amounts (and richly) to serve thee:
He did not heav'n and earth create,
Yet studies them, not him by whom they be.

Teach me thy love to know;
That this new light, which now I see,
May both the work and workman show:
Then by a sun-beam I will climb to thee.

Matins: the service of morning prayer in the Church of England. **Ope:** open. **Estate:** situation in life.

Savoring the poem. This beautiful poem begins with the recognition that God never sleeps. The moment we awake, he's there, ready to receive our prayers and praise. That's why the Herbert family attended morning (and evening) prayer services daily in the Bemerton church, across the road from their manse. What puzzles Herbert here is not that God *requires* his worship, but that he *desires* it. Doesn't God have bigger fish to fry? Why woo his heart? Sadly, he knows that God's suit frequently fails. Man's assiduous study of creation (Herbert the Cambridge scholar knew it well and tells of it in "The Pearl") often leaves him ignorant of the Creator. So as Herbert enters a new day, he pauses to request God's help. Like C. S. Lewis and his famous meditation in a toolshed, Herbert wants to do more than simply look *at* God's light. He wants to look *along* it to behold the glorious Son who secures every blessing through his crucifixion (note the pun on "sun-beam"). He wants to "make a match" with God.

Shepherded by the poem. Could the opening lines of this poem lead to a reshaping of our morning routines? It's normal to "ope our eyes" onto a phone, television, or computer, giving it our first, fresh attention of the day. Those headlines, sports scores, social media feeds, and email inboxes will take all we offer and then ask for more. They're "ready there to catch / My morning-soul and sacrifice." What if, instead, we open our eyes onto God, who worked for us while we slept? He's ready to meet us—not sell us stuff. He's offering himself—not taking whatever he can get. As we receive his word *first thing,* before we hear any other words, we may find our communion with him more focused and fruitful. God loves your "morning-soul." If you ask him, he'll teach you to see him everywhere you look. All day long, you'll be climbing sun-beams to him.

Evensong

Blest be the God of love,
Who gave us eyes, and light, and power this day,
Both to be busy, and to play.
But much more blest be God above,

Who gave me sight alone,
Which to himself he did deny:
For when he sees my ways, I die:
But I have got his son, and he hath none.

What have I brought thee home
For this thy love? have I discharg'd the debt,
Which this day's favor did beget?
I ran; but all I brought, was foam.

Thy diet, care, and cost
Do end in bubbles, balls of wind;
Of wind to thee whom I have crossed,
But balls of wild-fire to my troubled mind.

Evensong: another name for evening prayer, the Church of England's daily evening service. **Who gave me sight . . . which to himself he did deny:** God turns a blind eye to the sin of those who are in Christ, not counting it against them. **and he hath none:** God gave his Son Jesus over to death. **Thy diet, care, and cost . . . balls of wind:** God's provision for Herbert doesn't result in gain for God.

Yet still thou goest on,
And now with darkness closest weary eyes,
Saying to man, *It doth suffice:*
Henceforth repose; your work is done.

Thus in thy ebony box
Thou dost enclose us, till the day
Put our amendment in our way,
And give new wheels to our disorder'd clocks.

I muse, which shows more love,
The day or night: that is the gale, this th' harbor;
That is the walk, and this the arbor;
Or that the garden, this the grove.

My God, thou art all love.
Not one poor minute scapes thy breast,
But brings a favor from above;
And in this love, more than in bed, I rest.

Savoring the poem. Herbert is a generous poet: "Evensong" is personal but plenty roomy enough for us to share. (Note the interplay between "I/me/my" and "us/our"). Here's the situation: the day is drawing to a close and Herbert is taking stock. Though one scholar suggests that the

Ebony box: a poetic description of the darkness of night, perhaps with associations of a coffin.

lack of coincidence between meter and rhyme may simulate scattered, sleepy thoughts,[18] there's too much clarity and order here to believe that. A gorgeous chiasm (A-B-C-C-B-A) frames the poem in lines 1 and 32:

Blest
    God
        Love
        Love
    I
Rest

The first word ("blest") rhymes with the final one ("rest"). God receives Herbert's blessing (i.e., praise), and Herbert receives God's rest. God is praised for his love, and Herbert rests in God's love. Within that frame, it's safe to recall and confess the sins and failures of the day. They're painful ("balls of wild-fire to my troubled mind") but not disqualifying or disabling. In fact, Herbert soon moves on from his shortcomings to God's love. He muses whether day or night shows that love more clearly. He then forsakes the question as inconsequential, since it's *all* from love. And now, finally, it's time for sleep. He'll rest in divine love—far better than a Sleep Number mattress.

Shepherded by the poem. We all know that last hour of the day can quickly go sideways, surfacing guilt, regret, and shame. Should we obscure it in a haze of entertainment amnesia as we so often do? Herbert offers us something much better. As you prepare for sleep, bless the "God of love." Recall his enabling of every good deed this day. Celebrate his forgiveness for every bad one, and your relationship with his Son. Have you done that? Is the gospel sweet? Now confess today's sin without despair. Confession of sin and acknowledgment of failure wrapped in a celebration of grace isn't catastrophic. God's love was with you today. It's toward you tonight. *Rest* in it.

The Windows

Lord, how can man preach thy eternal word?
He is a brittle crazy glass:
Yet in thy temple thou dost him afford
This glorious and transcendent place,
To be a window, through thy grace.

But when thou dost anneal in glass thy story,
Making thy life to shine within
The holy Preacher's; then the light and glory
More rev'rend grows, & more doth win:
Which else shows watrish, bleak, & thin.

Doctrine and life, colors and light, in one
When they combine and mingle, bring
A strong regard and awe: but speech alone
Doth vanish like a flaring thing,
And in the ears, not conscience ring.

Crazy: full of flaws. **Anneal:** to burn colors into glass. **Rev'rend:** worthy of reverence. **Watrish:** pale, washed out, lacking in color.

Savoring the poem. Can a sinful man preach God's holy word? For Herbert, that was a highly personal question. He knew he didn't *deserve* to preach. In "The Priesthood" he says, "I am both foul and brittle; much unfit / To deal in holy Writ." But, as he describes in "Aaron" and "The Priesthood," he drew hope from the imputed righteousness of Christ and from Scripture's teaching that God's power is made perfect in weakness. Here, he raises the question again (this time concerning "man" generally, not just himself), and now his thought moves in a fresh direction. Working within the heart and habits of a preacher, God can transform an otherwise flawed and fragile life into flaming glass that holds the congregation's gaze and endures in their memories, bringing glory to God. The preacher's personal holiness really matters (see Herbert's *The Country Parson* for his passion to proclaim this truth). The gospel lived illumines the gospel preached.

Shepherded by the poem. Herbert's vision of preaching was a local one, in which the people of the parish could observe their pastor's daily life. He himself lived across the street from his church and regularly visited the homes of his parishioners. In the New Testament, both a teacher's words *and life* matter (1 Cor. 11:1; Phil. 3:17; 4:9; 2 Thess. 3:9; Heb. 13:7). What would Herbert make of our contemporary evangelical world of celebrity preachers, widely-disseminated digital sermons, and megachurches? What happens when the life on stage is the only one seen? Do the "speech alone" sermons of a stranger make it past the ears to the conscience? If you're a preacher in your church, it's good to ask: *Is my life in Christ resulting in a "strong regard and awe" among the people of my church?* If you're a parishioner, how might you encourage your pastor in his pursuit of personal holiness?

Trinity Sunday

Lord, who hast form'd me out of mud,
And hast redeem'd me through thy blood,
And sanctifi'd me to do good;

Purge all my sins done heretofore:
For I confess my heavy score,
And I will strive to sin no more.

Enrich my heart, mouth, hands in me,
With faith, with hope, with charity;
That I may run, rise, rest with thee.

Savoring the poem. This little gem, written for Trinity Sunday, playfully embodies what it says. It's about the triune God. So of course it's composed of three stanzas of three lines each. And, of course, the first stanza highlights the past, present, and future work of Father, Son, and Holy Spirit, with another temporal triplet in stanza 2 (this one having to do with sin). But wait, there's more! Stanza 3 doubles down (sorry—*triples* down) on what comes before. Each of the three

Trinity Sunday: the first Sunday after Pentecost, a day for celebrating the Father, Son, and Holy Spirit. **Charity:** love.

lines now sprouts a series of three (body parts, virtues, actions). This poem is dynamic—it *moves* and *overflows* as threes beget threes. All this three-play embodies and expresses the exuberant, world-creating, triune life of the God about whom Herbert writes. And there may be more. Notice that the lines of each stanza rhyme: each line unique, all unified. Is this a nod to God's three-in-one nature? Herbert is subtle and skillful enough to mean it. Let's not underrate this poem. Though diminutive in size, its scope encompasses a vast temporal expanse, from creation (in the first line) to new creation (in the last). The tip-off that the final line is about end-time realities (rather than our daily routines) is that "run" comes *before* "rise." We run our lifetime race (Heb. 12:1) and then rise to eternal rest with Christ.

Shepherded by the poem. The triune God holds the universe together. So it shouldn't surprise us that, whenever a robust Trinitarian theology is lacking, other problems tend to surface (such as an inadequate theology of the body or an insufficient doctrine of sanctification). In this Trinitarian poem, Herbert models a vision of the Christian life that exults in God's creation *and* redemption; his justifying *and* sanctifying work; our faith in him *and* our love for others. Are there ways your spiritual practice and prayers can become more fully Trinitarian?

Denial

When my devotions could not pierce
Thy silent ears;
Then was my heart broken, as was my verse;
My breast was full of fears
And disorder:

My bent thoughts, like a brittle bow,
Did fly asunder:
Each took his way; some would to pleasures go,
Some to the wars and thunder
Of alarms.

As good go any where, they say,
As to benumb
Both knees and heart, in crying night and day,
Come, come, my God, O come,
But no hearing.

O that thou shouldst give dust a tongue
To cry to thee,
And then not hear it crying! all day long
My heart was in my knee,
But no hearing.

A brittle bow: a fragile, easily broken weapon. This phrase may also refer to the bow of a stringed instrument, a meaning which finds support from the numerous musical references later in the poem.

Therefore my soul lay out of sight,
Untun'd, unstrung:
My feeble spirit, unable to look right,
Like a nipt blossom, hung
Discontented.

O cheer and tune my heartless breast,
Defer no time;
That so thy favors granting my request,
They and my mind may chime,
And mend my rhyme.

Savoring the poem. Observe the scattered lines of this poem. It's a visual mess—more chaotic than a teenager's room. Now read it aloud and hear its stilted rhythm. *What is wrong with this poem?* The final phrases in each stanza are especially awkward. Like a man wearing a tuxedo to a pool party, they don't fit in. Dangling awkwardly, they break both rhythm and rhyme. They're a pebble in the poem's shoe. *What is wrong with this poem?* It's not that Herbert was having an off-day. In line 3, he tells us exactly what's happening: "Then was my heart broken, as was my verse." The earthquake of divine silence and denial has shaken both Herbert and his poem, and the rubble is everywhere. So the erratic rhythm and broken rhyme is in fact Herbert's gift to us, allowing us to hear and feel in our bodies the lurching angst of a scattered heart struggling to

Nipt: archaic past tense of "nip," meaning to sever or injure (perhaps by frost). **Chime:** rhyme.

rest in a silent God. After providing that experience five times in a row, Herbert offers another gift. In the last stanza, the concluding words of the second and fourth lines finally rhyme with the last word of the fifth line, which is (appropriately enough!) "rhyme." So Herbert offers us a mini-experience of the very joy he's seeking throughout the poem: the satisfying, chiming beauty of God's provision perfectly matching our needs.

Shepherded by the poem. The seeming absence of God can be profoundly disorienting—Herbert's odd phrase in line 2, "Thy silent ears," hints at the confusion he himself feels (to state the obvious: ears aren't really silent). If you're in a season where God seems far away, your thoughts may be flying every which way. You may feel, like a battered violin at a yard sale, "Untun'd, unstrung." It may seem that the once-fresh blossom of your life has been severed from the stalk, leaving a drab, dull future. Herbert models for us a response that we see also in the psalms: keep pleading with God. Don't give up. In the memorable words of this poem, keep your heart in your knee all day long. *Come, come, my God, O come.* Wait for God to mend your rhyme.

Virtue

Sweet day, so cool, so calm, so bright,
The bridal of the earth and sky:
The dew shall weep thy fall to night;
For thou must die.

Sweet rose, whose hue angry and brave
Bids the rash gazer wipe his eye:
Thy root is ever in its grave
And thou must die.

Sweet spring, full of sweet days and roses,
A box where sweets compacted lie;
My music shows ye have your closes,
And all must die.

Only a sweet and virtuous soul,
Like season'd timber, never gives;
But though the whole world turn to coal,
Then chiefly lives.

Bridal: wedding, wedding feast. **Rash:** hasty, impetuous. **A box where sweets compacted lie:** a box filled with perfumes made from herbs or flowers. **Closes:** concluding musical phrases. **Gives:** gives way, warps.

Savoring the poem. If you've ever walked through a cool, sunny morning; or studied closely a gorgeous flower; or inhaled deeply the smell of fresh, tender grass, you know what Herbert is feeling in this poem. Our world is stunningly beautiful. We know that's how Herbert experiences it, because he sprinkles his favorite adjective ("sweet") all over this poem, like a man whose wife should hide the saltshaker. But now cue a minor key, because Herbert sees in creation itself—in the daily dew, the rose's root, the ending of a song—that it won't last. That solemn drumbeat "Thou must die" crescendos into stanza 3: "And all must die." And yet, not quite "all." Here's what Herbert wants us to know: virtuous souls are indestructible. They alone endure from this world to the next. And it's not that they just barely survive the fires of judgment, damaged and joyless forever. Rather they experience in that future world a *richer* life than any they've known before ("Then chiefly lives"). So what exactly is a virtuous soul and how does one gain it? One clear meaning of "virtue" is moral excellence—the opposite of vice. Herbert says a soul gains this moral excellence through seasoning, like wood that's grown strong by enduring all weathers for years. Suffering produces endurance, character, and hope (Rom. 5:3–5). Perhaps another meaning of "virtue" is at play in this poem. If 1 Peter 1:6–7, with its mention of "various trials" and "the tested genuineness of your faith," lies behind the imagery of seasoned timber, then "virtue" may refer to genuine, mature, enduring faith in Christ. The seasoned soul never gives. Instead, with God, it lives.

Shepherded by the poem. While Herbert closely observed and deeply appreciated the beauty of this world, he aimed to live always toward the world to come. Here's how he said it in "Man's Medley," referring to mankind's life in this world: "Not that he may not here / Taste of the cheer, / But as birds drink, and straight lift up their head, / So he must sip and think / Of better drink / He may attain to, after he is dead."

The blessings of this life whet our appetites for heaven, and the hardships weather us for eternity. How is God stoking your desire through pleasure? How is he seasoning your soul through pain? As you sip the pleasures of this world, are you lifting your head and longing for the better drink of heaven?

The Pearl. *Matth. 13.*

I know the ways of learning; both the head
And pipes that feed the press, and make it run;
What reason hath from nature borrowed,
Or of it self, like a good housewife, spun
In laws and policy; what the stars conspire,
What willing nature speaks, what forc'd by fire;
Both th' old discoveries, and the new-found seas,
The stock and surplus, cause and history:
All these stand open, or I have the keys:
Yet I love thee.

I know the ways of honor, what maintains
The quick returns of courtesy and wit:
In vies of favors whether party gains,
When glory swells the heart, and moldeth it
To all expressions both of hand and eye,
Which on the world a true-love-knot may tie,
And bear the bundle, wheresoe're it goes:
How many drams of spirit there must be
To sell my life unto my friends or foes:
Yet I love thee.

The head and pipes that feed the press: a reference to the workings of a printing press. **What the stars conspire:** what effects the stars together have on earth. **What willing nature . . . fire:** heating by fire is required to discover some properties of nature; others are immediately evident. **The stock and surplus:** old knowledge and new discoveries. **Vies:** competitions. **Drams of spirit:** measures of liquor.

I know the ways of pleasure, the sweet strains,
The lullings and the relishes of it;
The propositions of hot blood and brains;
What mirth and music mean; what love and wit
Have done these twenty hundred years, and more:
I know the projects of unbridled store:
My stuff is flesh, not brass; my senses live,
And grumble oft, that they have more in me
Than he that curbs them, being but one to five:
Yet I love thee.

I know all these, and have them in my hand:
Therefore not sealed, but with open eyes
I fly to thee, and fully understand
Both the main sale, and the commodities;
And at what rate and price I have thy love;
With all the circumstances that may move:
Yet through these labyrinths, not my groveling wit,
But thy silk twist let down from heav'n to me,
Did both conduct and teach me, how by it
To climb to thee.

Commodities: wares.

Savoring the poem. Jesus told a parable: "Again, the kingdom of heaven is like a merchant in search of fine pearls, who, on finding one pearl of great value, went and sold all that he had and bought it" (Matt. 13:45–46). "The Pearl" is Herbert's lived experience of that story. A celebrated scholar, he knew "the ways of learning." An aristocrat, he knew "the ways of honor." He had a refined aesthetic sense and skill in music, so he knew "the ways of pleasure." As a man, he experienced sexual longing—the imagery of "sweet strains, / The lullings and the relishes of it" is both musical and sexual.[19] And yet he desired the pearl. This poem's effectiveness runs on the contrast between its packed stanzas and persistent refrain ("Yet I love thee"). Which will tip the scales? We find out in the end. With open eyes, he sells all to buy the pearl. Lest this be misunderstood as boasting, the poem's fourth major "yet" (see lines 10, 20, 30, 37), together with an allusion to the myth of Theseus, in which it was Ariadne's thread that guided Theseus out of the labyrinth, gives credit where (all) credit is (ever) due. "The poem is evidence, finally, not of what man can do but of what God has done."[20]

Shepherded by the poem. God himself is the pearl ("I fly to thee"; "To climb to thee"). What did it actually mean for Herbert to sell all for the love of God? What does it mean for us? No simple answers here. In Herbert's case, the "main sale" of learning, honor, and pleasure seems to have been less a complete renunciation than a pervasive relativization; a demotion of each from supreme to secondary. After all, he continued to read and write theology, pen poems, play the lute, and benefit from rich relatives. When we weigh the sumptuous treasures of our lives against that slender "I love thee," which wins? How should we live in light of this? We best be asking God. He alone can cause our hearts to treasure him above all else (Pss. 63:3; 90:14).

Antiphon (2)

Chor. Praised be the God of love,
Men. Here below,
Angels. And here above:
Cho. Who hath dealt his mercies so,
Ang. To his friend,
Men. And to his foe;

Cho. That both grace and glory tend
Ang. Us of old,
Men. And us in th'end.
Cho. The great shepherd of the fold
Ang. Us did make,
Men. For us was sold.

Cho. He our foes in pieces brake;
Ang. Him we touch;
Men. And him we take.
Cho. Wherefore since that he is such,
Ang. We adore,
Men. And we do crouch.

Antiphon: a hymn or psalm sung or chanted in alternating, responsive parts. **Crouch:** bow in reverence.

Cho. Lord, thy praises should be more.
Men. We have none,
Ang. And we no store.
Cho. Praised be the God alone,
Who hath made of two folds one.

Savoring the poem. This is vintage Herbert, exploring cosmic realities and biblical themes (e.g., Ps. 8; John 10:16; 1 Pet. 1:12) with imaginative verve and deceptive simplicity (no word except the title exceeds two syllables). Praise of God is the subject (see the exhortations in lines 1 and 22), but the really interesting contribution (as we might have hoped, given the title) is an exploration of unity-in-diversity, of what *distinguishes* and *unites* men and angels in worship. Men are clearly at some disadvantage to angels. While both have received God's mercy, angels are his friends and men his foes. While God's grace tends both, angels are old-timers and men Johnny-come-latelies. However, surprisingly, the last become first. Yes, Christ made angels—but he was betrayed, sold, and crucified for men. Angels touch the one who breaks their foes, but Christ himself was broken *as* a foe for men, who "take" him at Holy Communion. Though important, these differences aren't the last word. The climactic focus is on *unity,* and here the poem does what it says. In the second half of the final stanza, men and angels unite for the first time in the poem to sing a common lyric rather than two separate parts, and the poem's triumphant concluding word is "one." Look what

Store: accumulated supply.

God has wrought! This antiphonal celebration is richer than anything one chorus could sing alone.

Shepherded by the poem. The church sings the doxology:

> Praise God from whom all blessings flow
> Praise him all creatures here below;
> Praise him above, ye heavenly host;
> Praise Father, Son, and Holy Ghost.
> Amen.

In doing so, it calls men and angels to worship, joining heaven and earth in praise. That's what Herbert does here. Remember this poem the next time you gather with your local church. Know that the congregation is larger than just those you can see. Join in heavenly worship.

Mortification

How soon doth man decay!
When clothes are taken from a chest of sweets
To swaddle infants, whose young breath
Scarce knows the way;
Those clouts are little winding sheets,
Which do consign and send them unto death.

When boys go first to bed,
They step into their voluntary graves,
Sleep binds them fast; only their breath
Makes them not dead;
Successive nights, like rolling waves,
Convey them quickly, who are bound for death.

When youth is frank and free,
And calls for music, while his veins do swell,
All day exchanging mirth and breath
In company;
That music summons to the knell,
Which shall befriend him at the hour of death.

Chest of sweets: a box for keeping linens with dried herbs and flowers inside to make the clothes fresh and sweet-swelling. **Clouts:** cloths. **Winding sheets:** shrouds in which a corpse is wrapped. **Knell:** tolling of a bell (often for a funeral).

When man grows staid and wise,
Getting a house and home, where he may move
Within the circle of his breath,
Schooling his eyes;
That dumb enclosure maketh love
Unto the coffin, that attends his death.

When age grows low and weak,
Marking his grave, and thawing ev'ry year,
Till all do melt, and drown his breath
When he would speak;
A chair or litter shows the bier,
Which shall convey him to the house of death.

Man, ere he is aware,
Hath put together a solemnity,
And drest his hearse, while he has breath
As yet to spare;
Yet Lord, instruct us so to die,
That all these dyings may be life in death.

Staid: respectable, unadventurous. **Schooling his eyes:** coming to learn self-control. **Dumb:** silent. **Maketh love unto the coffin:** the limited sphere of the respectable man resembles his silent future in the coffin. **Litter:** chair or bed with poles for carrying someone. **Bier:** stretcher for carrying a corpse to the grave. **Solemnity:** ceremonial procession (to the grave).

Savoring the poem. Some books and movies (including, famously, *The Sixth Sense*) hold a revelation for the end that transforms everything before. Watch for that here. While skillfully worked, "Mortification" seems at first a conventional-enough poem, pursuing a line of thought treated in other poetry of the time, and expanding on the *Book of Common Prayer*'s burial service, "In the midst of life we be in death." Herbert hears death's whispers in all life's stages. Swaddled infants, sleeping boys, partying teens, staid adults, weakened seniors—the signs are everywhere. If you listen carefully to the poem (noticing the words "breath" in the third line of each stanza and "death" in each fifth line), you can almost hear the inhalations and exhalations that take us to the grave.[21] So, of course, this poem (titled "Mortification," after all) is about death, right? Yes and no. In the last two lines, Herbert quite literally flips the script: from the *Book of Common Prayer*'s "death in life" to "life in death." The one who is the resurrection and the life makes death a door to life. And, of course, this transforms our reading of the entire poem. Fresh hope washes back over every stanza. On a second reading, it's all new: those hints of death are now steps toward life. Through this poem, Herbert offers a mini-experience of what is possible for all. For those who hope in God's new creation, it never holds its place in the future. It blesses backward, lighting the dark, keeping our heads above water.

Shepherded by the poem. Does the thought of illness and of your future death cause you anxiety? How might greater knowledge of, and excitement for, God's future new creation begin to transform your present experience? All of us can become students of the new creation, meditating on the Bible's teaching, listening to sermons and reading books that fuel desire for our final future. John beckoned his suffering readers to contemplate a future better than Eden, when every tear would be wiped away and death would be no more (Revelation 21–22). The apostle Paul's knowledge of what death would bring eliminated fear of it (Phil. 1:20–26). The same can be true for us. What's more, we can practice "mortification" today, seeking to kill the sin that would kill us, as the apostle Paul teaches. "For if you live according to the flesh you will die, but if by the Spirit you put to death the deeds of the body, you will live" (Rom. 8:13). May all our daily "dyings" to sin and self truly be "life in death" for us.

The Dawning

Awake sad heart, whom sorrow ever drowns;
    Take up thine eyes, which feed on earth;
Unfold thy forehead gather'd into frowns:
    Thy Savior comes, and with him mirth:
                    Awake, awake;
And with a thankful heart his comforts take.
    But thou dost still lament, and pine, and cry;
    And feel his death, but not his victory.

Arise sad heart; if thou dost not withstand,
    Christ's resurrection thine may be:
Do not by hanging down break from the hand,
    Which as it riseth, raiseth thee:
                    Arise, Arise;
And with his burial-linen dry thine eyes:
    Christ left his grave-clothes, that we might, when grief
    Draws tears, or blood, not want an handkerchief.

Take up thine eyes, which feed on earth: lift your downcast eyes.

Savoring the poem. Christianity is realistic and optimistic, and so is this Easter poem. Christ has risen! Rejoice! "Thy Savior comes, and with him mirth." Break out the party hats! And yet the poem is addressed to a "sad heart" (perhaps the poet's own) that laments, pines, and cries. There's no quick fix: the exhortations of the first stanza apparently don't have their intended effect ("But thou dost still lament . . ."). Here is a realistic depiction of life in a post-Easter, pre-heaven world. Easter inaugurates but does not consummate Christ's victory. The battle is won, but Satan does damage during the clean-up operation. Life can hurt so bad that we weep and bleed (line 16). This poem meets us in the tears and offers something much better than a pep talk. To see its rooted optimism, notice that the main exhortations, "awake" and "arise" (emphasized by their front-loaded positions in lines 1 and 9 and their repetition in lines 5 and 13), are what Jesus himself did on Easter Sunday morning. Because he awoke and arose, we don't need to raise ourselves. He'll do the work for us. "Do not by hanging down break from the hand, / Which as it riseth, raiseth thee." Christ gives blessing in a broken world. That's the point of Herbert's boldly creative and playful re-envisioning of the graveclothes as our handkerchief. He's left us all we need!

Shepherded by the poem. How do you tend to navigate this "already/not-yet" world? Do you sometimes give way to despair? Or are you more inclined to be overly optimistic and then crushed when things don't work out? Christ's resurrection provides a way of realism (so we're not surprised by disappointment) and optimism (so we don't sink down to despair). Grief and tears are an inevitable reality of this life. But our tearful eyes can be locked on a Savior who comforts us now and raises us to a better future.

JESU

JESU is in my heart, his sacred name
Is deeply carved there: but th'other week
A great affliction broke the little frame,
Ev'n all to pieces: which I went to seek:
And first I found the corner, where was *J*,
After, where *ES*, and next where *U* was graved.
When I had got these parcels, instantly
I sat me down to spell them, and perceived
That to my broken heart he was *I ease you*,
And to the whole is *J E S U*.

Savoring the poem. There's not much taste for allegory these days—to most of us, it seems too artificial and didactic. On first glance, this one appears cutesy and contrived. But reading poetry is about taking second, third, and fourth glances, and the more we examine "JESU," the better it gets. It looks like a kiddie pool, but best bring your scuba gear. Here's an essential thing to know about the title (and the poem): in Latin, and in typical Renaissance practice, the letters *I* and *J* weren't distinguished. So, "Jesu" and "Iesu" are identical. As he loves to do, Herbert teaches theology by telling a story. The name "Jesu" ("Iesu") was carved in his heart (note the allusion to 2 Cor. 3:3), but a "great affliction" broke it apart. When Herbert stooped to gather the fragments and sat to reassemble them, he saw before him on the table three pieces: *I*, *ES*, and *U*. He read them as a sentence: "I ease you." Upon reassembly, he once again saw the familiar name "Jesu." So here is an awesome mystery wrapped in a child's tale. In our affliction, Jesus reveals to us new depths of himself. We know his compassion and care as we simply never can apart from brokenness. We meet him in the "fellowship of his sufferings" (Phil. 3:10 KJV). Yes, he's Jesus to all. But he's "I ease you" when the lay-off is announced, the divorce is finalized, or the cancer is inoperable. Herbert could have just told us that, but instead he *shows* us, because he wants us to *experience* the surprise of unexpected meaning in apparent meaninglessness. If you can feel that in a tiny way in this tiny poem, maybe, just maybe, it's possible to live it next time the bottom falls out.

Shepherded by the poem. This little allegory can be your friend in suffering. Will you receive its invitation to know Christ more fully? Another Herbert poem, "Longing," reminds us of the advantage of a broken heart: there are extra pieces to cry to the Savior. "Lord JESU, hear my heart, / Which hath been broken now so long, / That ev'ry part / Hath got a tongue!" Will you cry to him more fervently?

Dialogue

Sweetest Savior, if my soul
　Were but worth the having,
Quickly should I then control
　Any thought of waiving.
But when all my care and pains
Cannot give the name of gains
To thy wretch so full of stains;
What delight or hope remains?

What, Child, is the balance thine,
　Thine the poise and measure?
If I say, Thou shalt be mine;
　Finger not my treasure.
What the gains in having thee
Do amount to, only he,
Who for man was sold, can see;
That transferr'd th'accounts to me.

But as I can see no merit,
　Leading to this favor:
So the way to fit me for it,
　Is beyond my savor.

Waiving: "withholding the offer of my soul."[22] **Cannot give the name of gains to thy wretch:** cannot make my soul worth having. **Savor:** knowledge, understanding.

As the reason then is thine;
So the way is none of mine:
I disclaim the whole design:
Sin disclaims and I resign.

That is all, if that I could
Get without repining;
And my clay, my creature, would
Follow my resigning.
That as I did freely part
With my glory and desert,
Left all joys to feel all smart—
Ah! no more: thou break'st my heart.

Savoring the poem. Alternate stanzas of regular type and italics show the back-and-forth between Herbert and Christ. With an impassioned interruption in line 32, Herbert claims the last word. But Christ wins the argument. The key to understanding where things end is seeing where they begin. Herbert bases his soul's worth on his good works, deems his performance inadequate, and therefore judges himself a "wretch," unworthy of Christ's interest. Christ, loving Herbert's soul from an overflow of grace, knows him as "my treasure." Herbert's heart sounds humble. It's not. He thinks he can earn salvation on his own. He can't. The attempt itself is his deepest sin. That arrogant independence pokes

Disclaim: deny a connection with. **Resign:** give up and surrender an argument, or one's privileges, rights. **Smart:** stinging pain.

through soon enough: notice he doesn't even bother to ask Christ's opinion before writing himself off (the question in stanza 1 is rhetorical, not real). In stanza 2, Christ gently (calling Herbert "Child") rebukes the pride. But Herbert doubles down. This time he renounces—"resigns"—both Christ's pursuit of him and their present dialogue. This is where works-righteousness gets him; like the prodigal's older brother, he's standing outside the party. But Christ has another move up his sleeve. What Herbert needs is not towering righteousness, but toppled pride. He must repent of the very attempt to earn salvation. So Christ pivots hard to the cross, and he does so through wordplay. When Herbert said, "I resign" (line 24), he meant he was done with the dialogue. But "resign" is what Christ himself did. For our salvation, he surrendered heavenly glory (line 28), feeling the sharp sting of sin (line 31). It was a precipitous descent (see Phil. 2:6–8 and Heb. 1–2). And this is what finally breaks Herbert, showing him sin and love, similar to "The Agony." He's worse than he thought he was—his problem isn't just bad deeds, but also the rebellion of approaching Christ on the basis of his deeds at all. The cross breaks him of this and blesses him with a new understanding of the loving heart of Christ. This is the starting place for true relationship with God. The older brother is welcomed into the party.

Shepherded by the poem. The Bible assures us of our value to God. But, ironically, the best way of seeing and feeling that value is not to focus on our sterling reputations, stunning accomplishments, successful children, or stellar resumes. Rather, it's to look *away* from ourselves to Christ. Robert Murray M'Cheyne advised his parishioners to take ten looks at Christ for every look at themselves. This poem demonstrates the surpassing, transforming value of seeing Christ's sacrifice for us. It humbles us and gives us hope. How might you keep Christ in the center of your attention today?

The Holdfast

I threatened to observe the strict decree
Of my dear God with all my power & might.
But I was told by one, it could not be;
Yet I might trust in God to be my light.

Then will I trust, said I, in him alone.
Nay, ev'n to trust in him, was also his:
We must confess that nothing is our own.
Then I confess that he my succor is:

But to have nought is ours, not to confess
That we have nought. I stood amaz'd at this,
Much troubled, till I heard a friend express,
That all things were more ours by being his.
What Adam had, and forfeited for all,
Christ keepeth now, who cannot fail or fall.

Holdfast: "A clamp or bolt . . . which holds together or supports a building" and "that which is persistent."[23] **Succor:** help, comfort. **Nought:** nothing.

Savoring the poem. God is sovereign, and here is a poem to ground our uncertain souls in that immovable bedrock. As usual, Herbert tells a story rather than simply propounding a doctrine. This poem's story details a series of his increasingly modest attempts to play some role in his own salvation: *obeying* God's law, *trusting* in God, at least *confessing* God as his help. At each turn, an unnamed interlocutor stymies his efforts. This amazes and troubles Herbert. Is there really nothing he can contribute to his salvation? The pivot in his understanding (and the central, fresh insight of the poem), comes in the words of a friend, as recounted in the final three lines. Our salvation is more, not less, secure for being fully in the hands of Christ, our "holdfast."

Does the sovereignty of God in salvation exclude all human responsibility and action? Some scholars think that's exactly what Herbert's unnamed interlocutor believes. In their view, he's the bad guy—an "extremist," a "dour and joyless figure," who drives Herbert toward a "spiritually starved, supine position," an "absolute absence of volition,"[24] and even reaches "the brink of nihilism."[25] But not so fast. If we read his words carefully, we'll see that the interlocutor isn't a hyper-Calvinist who denies all human agency. In fact, he says both that Herbert must trust in God (line 4) and that trust is God's (line 6); both that we must confess (line 7) and that it's not ours to confess (lines 9–10). He's teaching the biblical view that we can do nothing *unaided* to secure our salvation. We believe only as God grants belief (Acts 13:48). So the flow of this poem isn't error (the interlocutor's supposed hyper-Calvinism) corrected by truth (the Calvinism of the "friend" in line 11). Rather, it's *all* true. Herbert's interlocutor is a *good* guy. In fact, those climactic three lines are the pastoral, practical pay-off of what he has said. The path to sweet assurance (at the end of the poem) runs through surrender to God's sovereignty (in the first part). God our fortress—not our own flimsy selves—is the ground of our confidence. Our faith is not in our faith.

It's in his Son's atoning death, which is once-for-all and fully complete, securing eternal redemption for us (Heb. 9:11–12). He who cannot fail or fall sustains forever our communion with God.

Shepherded by the poem. How might the Bible's grounding of our assurance in God's sovereignty strengthen you today? Here's one path to let your mind and heart travel along. In John 6:37, Jesus says, "All that the Father gives me will come to me." In John 6:44, he says, "No one can come to me unless the Father who sent me draws him." Coming to Jesus means believing in him (John 6:35). So do you hear him taking away your ultimate self-determination? You'll only believe in Jesus if the Father gives and draws you to him. Lest you regret what you've lost, keep listening to Jesus to see what you gain. Jesus continues, in each of those verses: "And whoever comes to me I will never cast out" (John 6:37). "And I will raise him up on the last day" (John 6:44). His sovereignty secures our eternity. You're his forever. You will be raised. All things are more ours by being his.

The Bag

Away despair! my gracious Lord doth hear.
    Though winds and waves assault my keel,
    He doth preserve it: he doth steer,
    Ev'n when the boat seems most to reel.
    Storms are the triumph of his art:
Well may he close his eyes, but not his heart.

Hast thou not heard, that my Lord Jesus di'd?
    Then let me tell thee a strange story.
    The God of power, as he did ride
    In his majestic robes of glory,
    Resolv'd to light; and so one day
He did descend, undressing all the way.

The stars his tire of light and rings obtain'd,
    The cloud his bow, the fire his spear,
    The sky his azure mantle gain'd.
    And when they ask'd, what he would wear;
    He smil'd and said as he did go,
He had new clothes a making here below.

Keel: the central timber on the bottom of a boat. **Light:** alight, descend. **Tire:** attire. **Azure:** blue.

When he was come, as travellers are wont,
    He did repair unto an inn.
    Both then, and after, many a brunt
    He did endure to cancel sin:
    And having giv'n the rest before,
Here he gave up his life to pay our score.

But as he was returning, there came one
    That ran upon him with a spear.
    He, who came hither all alone,
    Bringing nor man, nor arms, nor fear,
    Receiv'd the blow upon his side,
And straight he turn'd, and to his brethren cry'd,

If ye have any thing to send or write,
    I have no bag, but here is room:
    Unto my Father's hands and sight,
    Believe me, it shall safely come.
    That I shall mind, what you impart;
Look, you may put it very near my heart.

Or if hereafter any of my friends
    Will use me in this kind, the door
    Shall still be open; what he sends
    I will present, and somewhat more,
    Not to his hurt. Sighs will convey
Any thing to me. Hark, Despair, away.

Brunt: attack, the force or shock of something. **Pay our score:** remove the debt of our sins.

Savoring the poem. Why are babies born with severe defects? Why are innocents murdered in brutal wars? Why do seniors die alone? Most of the suffering in this world is unexplained. Life doesn't come with an answer key. If a poet wants us to *feel* that (not just know it), how might he help us? Like the author of Psalm 88, he might end his poem dangling in despair, no facile answers offered. That's what Herbert does in "Longing" (the poem just before this one in *The Temple*), the final lines of which are: "And heal my troubled breast which cries, / Which dies." Herbert gives us a mini-experience of unresolved desolation. That's life.

But what if a poet also wants us to *feel* (not just know) that even sin-induced despair is part of a God-ordered world—that there's reality, but not finality, to our confusion? He might help us by embedding his despairing poem within a larger body of work. In the Psalter, Psalm 89 comes after Psalm 88. And in *The Temple*, "The Bag" comes after "Longing." Like a naughty dog told to go home, the despair expressed in "Longing" is rebuked and dismissed in the first and final lines of "The Bag." Go away! The dispeller of despair is Jesus, his eyes closed in the storm but his heart open toward us. That storm, it turns out, is the triumph of his art. And we know his heart is for us, because of what he's given up. In a bold, imaginative play on Philippians 2:5–11, Herbert envisions him descending from heaven, shedding wealth, weapons, garments, and glory. Surrendering his life. Speared in the side, the resulting hole forming a macabre mail bag with which he now delivers our messages to the Father. We are not forgotten. We are heard, known, and loved by a storm-stilling Savior. Despair, away!

Shepherded by the poem. Some followers of Christ tend to underplay the reality of sadness and confusion in a fallen world, rushing immediately to the relief Christ offers. Other Christians wallow in despair, not applying gospel truth. What are the dangers of each approach? Are you tempted toward one or the other? How does Herbert acknowledge both hardship and hope? How can this poem help you follow Christ in a Christless world? Next time you pray to the Father, it's worth pausing to consider what it cost Christ to convey your message, and how eager he is to receive and deliver even your inarticulate sighs. This is our Savior.

The Collar

I struck the board, and cry'd, No more.
I will abroad.
What? shall I ever sigh and pine?
My lines and life are free; free as the road,
Loose as the wind, as large as store.
Shall I be still in suit?
Have I no harvest but a thorn
To let me blood, and not restore
What I have lost with cordial fruit?
Sure there was wine
Before my sighs did dry it: there was corn
Before my tears did drown it.
Is the year only lost to me?
Have I no bays to crown it?
No flowers, no garlands gay? all blasted?
All wasted?
Not so, my heart: but there is fruit,
And thou hast hands.
Recover all thy sigh-blown age
On double pleasures: leave thy cold dispute

Board: table. **Lines:** lines of poetry; course of action. **Store:** supply of something kept for future use. **In suit:** petitioning; perhaps this also refers to the clerical suit, since the poem's title likely alludes to the clerical collar worn by priests. **Cordial:** comforting medicine. **Bays:** leaves of the poet's crown.

Of what is fit, and not. Forsake thy cage,
Thy rope of sands,
Which petty thoughts have made, and made to
thee
Good cable, to enforce and draw,
And be thy law,
While thou didst wink and wouldst not see.
Away; take heed:
I will abroad.
Call in thy death's head there: tie up thy fears.
He that forbears
To suit and serve his need,
Deserves his load.
But as I rav'd and grew more fierce and wild
At every word,
Me thoughts I heard one calling, *Child*:
And I reply'd, *My Lord*.

Savoring the poem. *Oof.* We're dropped abruptly into a moment of defiant decision. Herbert has had it. Life is too hard—long on sighs and tears, short on pleasure and reward. So, Jonah-like, he'll flee. "No more. / I will abroad." Begone all false notions of George Herbert, the pious parson of quiet Bemerton, the peaceful poet of quaint verse. God's

Rope of sands: proverbial phrase, describing "attempts at the impossible, or the object of fruitless activity."[26] **Good cable:** a strong cord formed of the petty thoughts that have bound him. **Death's head:** a skull, or some other reminder of mortality.

requirements (including perhaps his call of Herbert into the priesthood) are a confining collar around his neck, and he's fighting free. His instinct is to run (lines 1–16) and to have fun (lines 17–32), to evade pain and enjoy pleasure, to flee far and live hard. This is rebellion, and it's embodied in the odd look of the lines on the page, the irregular beat expressing his newfound independence ("My lines and life are free"). But is this really what freedom feels like? Disjointed, scattered, erratic? Herbert's self-talk (line 17) makes him no happier and takes him further from God. What he really needs to hear is not his own voice but the voice of another. That's what he now hears. Just one word ("Child") is enough. This new Caller (a play on the poem's title) invites him into the freedom and joy of sonship (Rom. 8:14–17). And with two words ("my Lord") Herbert accepts. Accordingly, the rhyme scheme clicks back into place in the final four lines, embodying the beauty of relationship with God. This is true freedom.

Shepherded by the poem. Have you, like Herbert, ever come to a point of frustration with life and rebellion against God? What was it like? Did your pursuit of "double pleasures" lead to the freedom and joy you were seeking? If God called you back, how did he do it? Are there areas of your life where you might now hear him calling, "Child"? Hear that not as castigation for childishness and foolishness but as his affirmation that, through Christ, you belong to him as his child (John 1:12–13). What will your response be?

The Call

Come, my Way, my Truth, my Life:
Such a Way, as gives us breath:
Such a Truth, as ends all strife:
Such a Life, as killeth death.

Come, my Light, my Feast, my Strength:
Such a Light, as shows a feast:
Such a Feast, as mends in length:
Such a Strength, as makes his guest.

Come, my Joy, my Love, my Heart:
Such a Joy, as none can move:
Such a Love, as none can part:
Such a Heart, as joys in love.

Savoring the poem. As the title suggests, and as "Come" at the head of each stanza shows, this poem is an invitation. Christ's presence is requested, his friendship celebrated (the threefold "my" in the first line of each stanza is a warm embrace), and his goodness described (note

Mends in length: Gets better as it goes.

the threefold "Such a . . ." in each stanza). So the poem is invitational, personal, and Christological. We may think it's so personal that there's no room for us in it. Not so. The "us" of line 2 opens a door for all who desire. We too can know, celebrate, and invite Christ. He can be for us the surprising way that *gives* breath (while other journeys leave us breathless). He can be for us the surprising feast that gets better as it goes (like the Cana wine that improved as the meal progressed, John 2:1–11). This poem contains an implicit call, an invitation to join Herbert's invitation of Christ. One final thought: Herbert's Christ is a sovereign Lord who grants spiritual life (line 2) and spiritual perception (line 6), who effectually draws (line 8) and keeps (lines 10–11) his own. So might this poem be about a divine call prior to, and more powerful than, Herbert's own?

Shepherded by the poem. Jesus invites us to come to him (Matt. 11:28–30). Are we reciprocating with regular invitations for him to come to us? The Bible ends this way: "Come, Lord Jesus!" (Rev. 22:20). This exquisite little poem models how meditation on Christ's goodness leads naturally to desires for closer communion with him. Let's freely express those desires to him and trust him to respond. He's already at the door, ready to break bread together (Rev. 3:20).

Joseph's Coat

Wounded I sing, tormented I indite,
Thrown down I fall into a bed, and rest:
Sorrow hath chang'd its note: such is his will,
Who changeth all things, as him pleaseth best.
   For well he knows, if but one grief and smart
Among my many had his full career,
Sure it would carrie with it ev'n my heart,
And both would run untill they found a bier
   To fetch the body; both being due to grief.
But he hath spoil'd the race; and giv'n to anguish
One of Joy's coats, 'ticing it with relief
To linger in me, and together languish.
   I live to show his power, who once did bring
   My *joys* to *weep*, and now my *griefs* to *sing*.

Savoring the poem. Although Herbert was a weak and wounded man—often sick, anxious, uncertain, struggling—things seem to be looking up a bit at the beginning of this poem. Following a season of struggle, he's again singing, writing, and resting. He attributes this to the sovereign

Indite: write, compose. **Smart:** sharp pain. **Had his full career:** could proceed without interruption. **Bier:** stretcher for carrying a corpse to the grave. **'Ticing:** enticing.

God who "changeth all things, as him pleaseth best." God does whatever he chooses, answering to no one, often surprising us—just as we're surprised (on a much more trivial level) by the failure of the word "will" in line 3 to fit the sonnet's expected rhyme scheme. As usual, Herbert has this poem doing what it's saying, because that drives the point deeper. And the surprises continue as we move along. Why did God improve Herbert's circumstances, granting him "One of Joy's coats"? It was to spare him from overwhelming grief, which would have made him run for the grave. God was keeping him alive. But there was another reason. Herbert says God provided joy in order to entice anguish "to linger in me," so that both joy and anguish would, simultaneously, be his experience. This is strange. Why does God want that? We get a clue in the poem's title, which recalls Jacob's famous gift to his favorite son: a coat of many colors. Whenever Joseph dressed, he donned his father's love. Herbert knows the same is true for him as he wears his mixed coat of joy and anguish. It's not divine carelessness or cruelty, but rather a gift of love to a cherished son. Joy's weeping produces humble dependence; grief's singing preserves from despair. That's why Herbert now lives to show God's power—because the sovereign, loving God grants him exactly what he needs.

Shepherded by the poem. The Heidelberg Catechism memorably and beautifully defines God's providence this way:

> The Almighty and everywhere present power of God; whereby, as it were, by his hand, he upholds and governs heaven, earth, and all creatures; so that herbs and grass, rain and drought, fruitful and barren years, meat and drink, health and sickness, riches and poverty, yea all things come not by chance, but by his fatherly hand.

He's in control of all of it. And it comes from his *fatherly* hand. He lovingly brings weakness and hardship into our lives, undermining self-sufficiency and sinful pride. And he "comforts us in all our affliction" (2 Cor. 1:4), sometimes even delivering us out of the suffering. Do you trust him to know what you need today? As your joys weep and your griefs sing, will you live to show his power? What does that actually look like for you in your present circumstances?

The Pulley

When God at first made man,
Having a glass of blessings standing by;
Let us (said he) pour on him all we can:
Let the world's riches, which dispersed lie,
Contract into a span.

So strength first made a way;
Then beauty flow'd, then wisdom, honor, pleasure:
When almost all was out, God made a stay,
Perceiving that alone of all his treasure
Rest in the bottom lay.

For if I should (said he)
Bestow this jewel also on my creature,
He would adore my gifts in stead of me,
And rest in Nature, not the God of Nature:
So both should losers be.

Yet let him keep the rest,
But keep them with repining restlessness:
Let him be rich and weary, that at least,
If goodness lead him not, yet weariness
May toss him to my breast.

Contract into a span: be gathered into the period of a human life. **Made a stay:** stopped, paused.

Savoring the poem. Augustine famously prayed to God, "You have made us for yourself, and our heart is restless till it finds its rest in you."[27] Herbert greatly appreciated Augustine, and "The Pulley" is his bold reimagining of the creation account of Genesis 1–2 in an Augustinian mode. Why does no good gift in this world—including spouse, children, possessions, accomplishments, reputation, friends, or health—ultimately satisfy? Herbert's answer: divine design. From the very beginning, God meant it to be that way. His lavish love blessed humanity with "the rest" (line 16)—that is, every good gift apart from "rest" (line 10)! *Yes* to strength, beauty, wisdom, honor, pleasure. But *no*, for now, to "rest" in the sense of ultimate joy, lasting satisfaction, settled peace, and final repose. Paradoxically, God's withholding is his greatest gift. Like a pulley, which draws heavy objects upward by downward force, so the drag of our "repining restlessness" may toss us to the breast of God.

Shepherded by the poem. There is clearly such a thing as sinful dissatisfaction—the boss whose employees can never work hard enough, the father whose kids will never please him, the greedy person who always wants more and better stuff. Neither Herbert nor the Bible endorse that kind of restlessness. But there's another kind of dissatisfaction—the kind C. S. Lewis was thinking of when he said, "If I find in myself a desire which no experience in this world can satisfy, the most probable explanation is that I was made for another world."[28] Do you sometimes feel this "repining restlessness," this longing for something more than you've yet found? How might you follow that tug toward more of God?

The Flower

How fresh, O Lord, how sweet and clean
Are thy returns! ev'n as the flowers in spring;
To which, besides their own demean,
The late-past frosts tributes of pleasure bring.
Grief melts away
Like snow in May,
As if there were no such cold thing.

Who would have thought my shrivel'd heart
Could have recover'd greenness? It was gone
Quite under ground; as flowers depart
To see their mother-root, when they have blown;
Where they together
All the hard weather,
Dead to the world, keep house unknown.

These are thy wonders, Lord of power,
Killing and quickning, bringing down to hell
And up to heaven in an hour;
Making a chiming of a passing-bell,
We say amiss,
This or that is:
Thy word is all, if we could spell.

Returns: revisitings. **Demean:** demeanor, bearing. **Blown:** blossomed. **Quickning:** making alive. **Making a chiming of a passing-bell:** changing a funeral bell into the sound of celebration. **Spell:** read correctly.

O that I once past changing were;
Fast in thy Paradise, where no flower can wither!
Many a spring I shoot up fair,
Offring at heav'n, growing and groaning thither:
Nor doth my flower
Want a spring-shower,
My sins and I joining together;

But while I grow to a straight line;
Still upwards bent, as if heav'n were mine own,
Thy anger comes, and I decline:
What frost to that? what pole is not the zone,
Where all things burn,
When thou dost turn,
And the least frown of thine is shown?

And now in age I bud again,
After so many deaths I live and write;
I once more smell the dew and rain,
And relish versing: O my only light,
It cannot be
That I am he
On whom thy tempests fell all night.

Fast: secure. **Want:** lack. **Versing:** writing poetry.

These are thy wonders, Lord of love,
To make us see we are but flowers that glide:
Which when we once can find and prove,
Thou hast a garden for us, where to bide.
Who would be more,
Swelling through store,
Forfeit their Paradise by their pride.

Savoring the poem. In *The Temple,* Herbert's poem "The Crosse" comes just before "The Flower" and expresses his submission to God, even when his heart is crushed and cut. *Thy will be done* (Matt. 6:10; 26:42 KJV). Sometimes life is a cross to bear. But sometimes God lets up. Sometimes he melts grief, awakening gladness. "Weeping may tarry for the night, but joy comes with the morning" (Ps. 30:5). "The Flower" is about that experience. Herbert is the flower. It's been a long, hard winter of suffering (stanza 2). It was his own fault: his sinful pride brought God's rebuke (stanza 5). But now the spring has come. God is near (stanzas 1, 6). Herbert can hardly believe it. He seems almost a different person—his senses alive, his delight in writing poetry reawakened. "O my only light, / It cannot be / That I am he / On whom thy tempests fell all night." And now he reflects on it all. Of course, he'd rather be planted in paradise, beyond all change (stanza 4). But he knows the "Lord of power" controls his ups and downs (stanza 3). And he knows two other things. First, as hard winters increase the pleasure of green

Glide: fade imperceptibly away. **Bide:** abide. **Store:** quantity or supply of something.

springs, so the disciplinary absence of God makes his returns all the sweeter (stanza 1). Second, God's purposes are good. He's the "Lord of love" (stanza 7). His chastening humbles our pride, teaching us "we are but flowers that glide," and because the path to the garden-paradise is humility, the way up is down. He's taking us to heaven. The grief is good. Notice the shape of the stanzas, each thinning in lines 5–6, swelling in line 7, embodying the poem's emphasis on restoration. This poem does what it says. Feel it fill.

Shepherded by the poem. John Drury calls "The Flower" a "supremely beautiful lyric of convalescence."[29] It's intensely personal. But notice the "I/my" of stanzas 1–6 opening up into the "we/us" of stanza 7. Herbert invites us into his experience. This is about us too. Do you recall times you came through hardship and suffering into a fresh awareness of God's presence and love? How did it feel? Would you describe it as Herbert does or in other ways? What did God teach you through those experiences? How can these reflections strengthen and encourage you in the present?

A True Hymn

My joy, my life, my crown!
My heart was meaning all the day,
Somewhat it fain would say:
And still it runneth mutt'ring up and down
With only this, *My joy, my life, my crown.*

Yet slight not these few words:
If truly said, they may take part
Among the best in art.
The fineness which a hymn or psalm affords,
Is, when the soul unto the lines accords.

He who craves all the mind,
And all the soul, and strength, and time,
If the words only rhyme,
Justly complains, that somewhat is behind
To make his verse, or write a hymn in kind.

Whereas if th' heart be moved,
Although the verse be somewhat scant,
God doth supply the want.
As when th' heart says (sighing to be approved)
O, could I love! And stops: God writeth, *Loved.*

Fain: gladly. **Scant:** poor, deficient in quality. **Want:** lack.

Savoring the poem. Herbert was close to God, and this poem gets us close to Herbert—right into his head and heart. We see him communing with God through repetition of a simple phrase. We know he delighted in this spiritual practice. According to "The Posy," he would sometimes sing or say throughout the day, "Less than the least of all God's mercies." Other times, over and over, "Thou art still my God," from "The Forerunners." Or, as in this poem, "My joy, my life, my crown." Just those simple words. They're enough, says this careful craftsman of language, this master of meter and rhyme, this greatest of spiritual poets—because hearts trump words. Don't miss the exquisite beauty of a singer and a simple hymn in sync. God craves consonance between lines and speaker. He means for us to mean our words because what he really wants is us (Luke 10:27). He can more than make up for our weak words. Of course he can. He spoke all things into being, and he'll gladly supplement scant verse when it's sincere. Here's how we know: consider a tender heart yearning to love him (to be loved *by* him). God fills all lack, satisfies all need, by saying, *Loved.* "We love him, because he first loved us" (1 John 4:19 KJV). Our words matter. Our hearts matter more. And our hearts can rest in this: God gets the last word.

Shepherded by the poem. Do you ever struggle with feeling you're not very gifted? With wishing you had more to offer? Gifting is great, but God doesn't require great gifting. He desires true worship. So let's give God what he wants. Let him supply the shortfall. Notice the weak rhyme (through verbal repetition) between lines 1 and 5. That's not like Herbert, who usually selects and sets his words with a jeweler's precision. Perhaps he's intentionally exemplifying poetic weakness, embodying his point that a sincere C- surpasses an empty A+. Let's take the hint. Give God the best you've got and your heart along with it. What will you offer him today?

The Answer

My comforts drop and melt away like snow:
I shake my head, and all the thoughts and ends,
Which my fierce youth did bandy, fall and flow
Like leaves about me: or like summer friends,
Flies of estates and sun-shine. But to all,
Who think me eager, hot, and undertaking,
But in my prosecutions slack and small;
As a young exhalation, newly waking,
Scorns his first bed of dirt, and means the sky;
But cooling by the way, grows pursy and slow,
And settling to a cloud, doth live and die
In that dark state of tears: to all, that so
    Show me, and set me, I have one reply,
    Which they that know the rest, know more than I.

Savoring the poem. Life has gone sideways, and this unsettled sonnet tells the tale. Comforts melt like spring snow. Youthful dreams scatter as autumn leaves. The best-laid plans, like fair-weather friends, or

Bandy: gather together, talk about. **Prosecutions:** course of action. **Exhalation:** a mist from damp ground. **Pursy:** short of breath, asthmatic, fat, swollen. **Show me, and set me:** depict me, and define me with a particular reputation.

fat flies in sunshine, buzz off. Who of us (if we've lived a while) can't identify with this situation? But Herbert's comedown has been unusually precipitous—from the public oratorship of Cambridge University (with aspirations toward the king's court) to unsettled years (ending in tiny Bemerton). He began, like water vapor, rising toward the heavens. Then settled like a cloud and fell like rain. Others wonder, others judge. "I have heard sober men censure him as a man that did not manage his brave parts to his best advantage and preferment, but lost himself in an humble way."[30] And so Herbert makes his one reply: "Which they that know the rest, know more than I." Of course, that's a non-answer. The poem's title is ironic. That unfinished last line embodies the wavering state of his uncertain life. The poem dangles because his story does. He doesn't know the rest of his reply because he doesn't know the rest of his life. We love Herbert for this honesty and humility. We love him for writing this unfinished poem. He speaks to us by speaking for us. Although it's scary to admit, we don't know the rest of our stories any more than he knows the rest of his.

Shepherded by the poem. The final line of this poem is great art: original, disarming, surprising, and honest. Often God uses our weaknesses and disappointments to prepare us for a contribution we could never otherwise make. He did it for Herbert. How might your unfinished, uncertain story—including those disappointed dreams that have blown clear away—become a means of encouraging others? Who can you encourage today?

Bitter-sweet

Ah my dear angry Lord,
Since thou dost love, yet strike;
Cast down, yet help afford;
Sure I will do the like.

I will complain, yet praise;
I will bewail, approve:
And all my sour-sweet days
I will lament, and love.

Savoring the poem. Please pull down firmly on the lap bar and remove all loose articles when boarding the roller coaster of the Christian life. There will be high highs, low lows, hair-raising loops, and stomach-churning corkscrews. Why so many twists and turns? Why the mingling of such pleasure and pain? Here's the bipartite reason for the bittersweet flavor: God's splendid purity and our polluting sin. He's holy and good; he loves and helps his own. But we're sinful and rebellious; so, he strikes and casts down. He's simultaneously "dear" and "angry." Accordingly, Herbert will respond with parallel paradoxicality. All his "sour-sweet"

Afford: provide, supply. **Complain:** grumble, lament.

days, he'll complain yet praise, bewail yet approve, lament and love (lines 5–8). Here's life in the "already / not-yet" kingdom, between the cross and the crown, "sorrowful, yet always rejoicing" (2 Cor. 6:10), realistic and reverent. Expressed in an economical eight lines, in words of at most two syllables, this miniature masterpiece is a guide to life in the present age.

Shepherded by the poem. Do you see your own experience reflected in these eight lines? How would you describe your "sour-sweet" days? When has *Ah* been drawn from your lips? Why is it important that Herbert commits both to complain and praise, bewail and approve, lament and love? What's the fruit of keeping these responses together? What results from expressing only one?

The Glance

When first thy sweet and gracious eye
Vouchsaf'd ev'n in the midst of youth and night
To look upon me, who before did lie
Weltring in sin;
I felt a sugred strange delight,
Passing all cordials made by any art,
Bedew, embalm, and overrun my heart,
And take it in.

Since that time many a bitter storm
My soul hath felt, ev'n able to destroy,
Had the malicious and ill-meaning harm
His swing and sway:
But still thy sweet original joy,
Sprung from thine eye, did work within my soul,
And surging griefs, when they grew bold, control,
And got the day.

If thy first glance so powerful be,
A mirth but open'd and seal'd up again;
What wonders shall we feel, when we shall see
Thy full-ey'd love!

Vouchsaf'd: was graciously willing. **Weltring:** wallowing. **Cordials:** comforting, pleasant-tasting medicines that were "thought to invigorate the heart, stimulate the circulation."[31] **Bedew, embalm, and overrun:** moisten gently like dew, anoint with sweet-smelling oil, pour over.

When thou shalt look us out of pain,
And one aspect of thine spend in delight
More than a thousand suns disburse in light,
In heav'n above.

Savoring the poem. There are many reasons to love Herbert's lyric verse. One is the sheer embodied beauty of his language. Go on, enjoy these words before you fully understand them. Experience the poem through your eyes and ears before you analyze it in your head. Feel the frisson of "a sugar'd strange delight" and the powerful, rolling "swing and sway" of an "ill-meaning harm." Even if you don't know exactly what "full-ey'd love" is, doesn't it sound like what you were made for? Don't you yearn for God to "look us out of pain"? This poem is meant not just to educate but to enthrall. And, of course, the poem itself is *about* delight—God's sovereign gift of an enlivening, encompassing joy greater than any Herbert had known, a "sweet original joy, / Sprung from thine eye," superior to all hardship and grief. Note the prodigality of God's love, manifest through words like "passing all," "overrun," and "powerful." And this overflowing goodness (Rom. 15:13; 2 Cor. 8:2) is just a foretaste of even greater things to come. In the final stanza, Herbert's imagination soars. That first, momentary glance overcame and sustained him, so what will the full, final, unfading gaze of God be like? What wonder, relief, and joy, flowing from a love greater than a thousand suns? This delightful poem about delight offers an *experience*

Aspect: face, position (of the heavenly bodies).

of its content. It does what it says. In Herbert's own words from "The Forerunners": "Beauty and beauteous words should go together." Don't you want to experience more of both?

Shepherded by the poem. The poem's title refers to God's sovereign, saving, sustaining gaze. *His* look is the one that counts. Perhaps the title nods also to Herbert's own glance forward in time, his delighted speculation regarding God's future, "full-ey'd love." Do you ever contemplate the goodness of God's final future for you? In Marilynne Robinson's novel *Gilead,* the old minister Boughton multiplies the pleasures of this world by two to get some sense of heaven. (He'd multiply by ten or twelve if he had the energy.) How might God's past faithfulness sharpen your desire for what's to come in the new creation? How might you become more heavenly-minded?

Aaron

Holiness on the head,
Light and perfections on the breast,
Harmonious bells below, raising the dead
To lead them unto life and rest.
Thus are true Aarons drest.

Profaneness in my head,
Defects and darkness in my breast,
A noise of passions ringing me for dead
Unto a place where is no rest.
Poor priest thus am I drest.

Only another head
I have, another heart and breast,
Another music, making live not dead,
Without whom I could have no rest:
In him I am well drest.

Christ is my only head,
My alone only heart and breast,
My only music, striking me ev'n dead;
That to the old man I may rest,
And be in him new drest.

Drest: dressed. **Profaneness:** unholiness. **Unto a place where is no rest:** hell.

So holy in my head,
Perfect and light in my dear breast,
My doctrine tun'd by Christ, (who is not dead,
But lives in me while I do rest)
Come people; Aaron's drest.

Savoring the poem. To feel the impact of this poem, imagine Herbert crossing the street from the Bemerton manse to his small village church. It's early Sunday morning and the congregation will arrive for worship in an hour or two. He longs to lead them well but knows he's woefully inadequate. Far from the holiness, purity, and beauty of the high priest Aaron, his own head and heart are profane, defective, and dark. He feels the danger not only of being a "poor priest" to others, but also of falling to hell himself. *What to do, what to do?* But now, in the silent sanctuary, there's a subtle shift. His focus moves from himself toward "another" (note the repeated use of that word in stanza 3) in whom he is "well drest." Who is this one? He's named as Christ in stanza 4—this time not simply as "another," but as Herbert's "only head" and "alone only heart and breast." Here is the Reformation teaching of the imputed righteousness of Christ. Herbert doesn't just hold it as a belief—he holds *onto* it for dear life. In many ways, nothing has changed. He's still the same inadequate pastor. But *everything* has changed, because he knows Christ's perfection is his. This is Luther's *simul justus et peccator*: simultaneously just and a sinner. And it's so important that Herbert wants you to taste it. To that end, he embeds within this poem a mini-experience of nothing and everything changing. The poem does what it says. Look carefully and you'll see it. Notice that the same sequence of words ends the five lines of each stanza. There's stasis throughout: head – breast – dead – rest – drest. Nothing changes. But now follow the stanzas from top to bottom and watch the (same) words fill with fresh meaning. *Everything* changes. The villagers will soon arrive for worship. And Herbert is ready, clothed with Christ's righteousness. It grounds his confidence, gives him rest, and guides his ringing invitation: "Come people; Aaron's drest."

Shepherded by the poem. In what areas of your life do you especially see your own sin? Where do you feel particular shame? Are there places, responsibilities, or relationships in which you feel perpetually inadequate? Up to this point, what has been your strategy for dealing with all that sin, shame, and inadequacy? This poem invites us to look to "another." How will the perfection of Christ ground your confidence today?

The Forerunners

The harbingers are come. See, see their mark;
White is their color, and behold my head.
But must they have my brain? must they dispark
Those sparkling notions, which therein were bred?
        Must dulness turn me to a clod?
Yet have they left me, *Thou art still my God.*

Good men ye be, to leave me my best room,
Ev'n all my heart, and what is lodged there:
I pass not, I, what of the rest become,
So *Thou art still my God,* be out of fear.
        He will be pleased with that ditty;
And if I please him, I write fine and witty.

Farewell sweet phrases, lovely metaphors.
But will ye leave me thus? when ye before
Of stews and brothels only knew the doors,
Then did I wash you with my tears, and more,
        Brought you to Church well drest and clad:
My God must have my best, ev'n all I had.

Harbinger: forerunner; one who goes before royal visitors, marking with chalk the doors of homes for them to lodge in (see lines 1–2, 35). **Dispark:** send animals out of a park; convert a park to another use. **Clod:** fool, blockhead. **Pass:** care. **Stews:** brothels.

Lovely enchanting language, sugar-cane,
Honey of roses, whither wilt thou fly?
Hath some fond lover tic'd thee to thy bane?
And wilt thou leave the Church, and love a sty?
        Fie, thou wilt soil thy broider'd coat,
And hurt thyself, and him that sings the note.

Let foolish lovers, if they will love dung,
And canvas, not with arras, clothe their shame:
Let folly speak in her own native tongue.
True beauty dwells on high: ours is a flame
        But borrow'd thence to light us thither.
Beauty and beauteous words should go together.

Yet if you go, I pass not; take your way:
For, *Thou art still my God,* is all that ye
Perhaps with more embellishment can say,
Go birds of spring: let winter have his fee,
        Let a bleak paleness chalk the door,
So all within be livelier than before.

Savoring the poem. Herbert had never been a robustly healthy man and would die before his fortieth birthday. In an age of short lifespans, he (presciently) counted his white hairs as forerunners of death. Tell-

Bane: curse, woe, cause of harm. **Fie:** exclamation of outrage or disgust. **Broider'd:** embroidered. **Arras:** rich tapestry material.

ingly, his keenest concern was the loss of mental acuity; more telling still, his clearest comfort was a heart for God, expressed in the phrase "Thou art still my God" (likely drawn from Ps. 31:14). This relationship (not poetry) was the center of his being, and he knew God would welcome even sub-par lines expressing his love. Good thing too, since lines 11–12 are a clearly (and intentionally) inferior couplet. Still, it was with sadness that he bid farewell to his "sweet phrases, lovely metaphors / . . . Lovely enchanting language, sugar-cane, / Honey of roses." He had placed those gorgeous words, often employed in secular love poetry, in the service of God. (Note the imagery of rescuing, washing, and dressing prostitutes, then bringing them to church.) It grieved him to imagine the beautiful words deserting the pews for the pigsty. Base realities expressed beautifully? It shouldn't be so. Beauty befits beauty. But in the end, he accepted the disparking of his sparkling notions for all his verse had elaborated on this one central truth: *Thou art still my God*. He could accept the winter of impending death so long as his heart kept burning bright.

Shepherded by the poem. A great artist grapples with the loss of his art. It's hard. But as his skill fades, his heart holds. How about us? How central to our identity is our gifting, our career, our productivity? Are they expressions and expansions of our love for God? Or have they usurped his place? Here's an opportunity for repentance, reconsideration, and reconsecration. Here also is a concise and compelling theology of beauty. Herbert expresses its divine origin ("True beauty dwells on high"), high purpose ("ours is a flame / But borrow'd thence to light us thither"), and proper context ("Beauty and beauteous words should go together").

The Elixir

Teach me, my God and King,
In all things thee to see,
And what I do in any thing,
To do it as for thee:

Not rudely, as a beast,
To run into an action;
But still to make thee prepossest,
And give it his perfection.

A man that looks on glass,
On it may stay his eye;
Or if he pleaseth, through it pass,
And then the heav'n espy.

All may of thee partake:
Nothing can be so mean,
Which with his tincture (for thy sake)
Will not grow bright and clean.

Elixir: a substance used by alchemists to change base metals to gold. **Rudely:** roughly, ignorantly, without thought. **Prepossest:** having a prior claim to something. **Tincture:** dye.

A servant with this clause
Makes drudgery divine:
Who sweeps a room, as for thy laws,
Makes that and th' action fine.

This is the famous stone
That turneth all to gold:
For that which God doth touch and own
Cannot for less be told.

Savoring the poem. Imagine discovering an elixir, a philosopher's stone, that transformed base metals into gold. Your world would change overnight—among other things, there'd soon be a lot less base metal and a lot more gold in it! That dream of magical transformation and limitless wealth has motivated people for centuries. But Herbert believes he knows something far better. *His* elixir will affect every conceivable (non-sinful) action within the field of human endeavor, filling each with purpose, pleasure, and purity. Imagine finding meaning in the mundane (changing a diaper, making a meal, and washing the dishes). The elixir can do that for you. Imagine fresh pleasure in figuring your taxes, walking your dog, and carrying out the trash. The elixir can do that too. Imagine having pure (not prideful) motives for your daily doings. Yes, the elixir can also make that so. And it's available for all, even the humblest servant doing the lowliest task. What is this world-transforming

The famous stone: the philosopher's stone.

wonder? Just a short clause: "For thy sake." We do ordinary things for our extraordinary God. We've got to mean the words "For thy sake" in order for them to work (hence Herbert's request for God to *teach* him). And they're effective because they align with reality; God really does "touch and own" everything. That's why there's no insignificant task, person, career, family, church, or place. It all matters. It's all a window through which we may view the unimaginable splendor of God himself ("In all things thee to see"). Perhaps it's not coincidental that Herbert shares this magnificent truth in a poem with a rather plain, unimpressive form and meter. Maybe this poem is itself an example of a wonder more extraordinary than it appears.

Shepherded by the poem. Do you have a good supply of elixir for your commute? For the repetitive tasks of parenting young children? For your volunteer hours at church? Make sure to stock up. What about posting the simple phrase "For thy sake" on your fridge, over your sink, on your dashboard, at your cubicle, or as your phone lockscreen? The Anglican church observes a Feast Day for George Herbert on February 27, and we'll do well to make its prayer our own:

> Our God and King, who called your servant George Herbert from the pursuit of worldly honors to be a pastor of souls, a poet, and a priest in your temple: Give unto us the grace, we pray, joyfully to perform the tasks you give us to do, knowing that nothing is menial or common that is done for your sake; through Jesus Christ our Lord, who lives and reigns with you and the Holy Spirit, one God, for ever and ever.

Death

Death, thou wast once an uncouth hideous thing,
Nothing but bones,
The sad effect of sadder groans;
Thy mouth was open, but thou couldst not sing.

For we consider'd thee as at some six
Or ten years hence,
After the loss of life and sense,
Flesh being turn'd to dust, and bones to sticks.

We look'd on this side of thee, shooting short;
Where we did find
The shells of fledge souls left behind,
Dry dust, which sheds no tears, but may extort.

But since our Savior's death did put some blood
Into thy face;
Thou art grown fair and full of grace,
Much in request, much sought for as a good.

Hence: in the future. **Fledge:** fully plumed young birds able to fly. **Extort:** obtain by force or intimidation.

For we do now behold thee gay and glad,
As at dooms-day;
When souls shall wear their new array,
And all thy bones with beauty shall be clad.

Therefore we can go die as sleep, and trust
Half that we have
Unto an honest faithful grave;
Making our pillows either down, or dust.

Savoring the poem. The apostle Paul derided death (1 Cor. 15:55). In this poem, Herbert pities it, humorously mocks it (scoffing at its skull's slack, silent mouth) and even compliments it (you're better-looking than I first thought). Our Savior's death is the poem's pivot. Before the cross, death's transformation of flesh to dust, and bones to sticks, defined it. We viewed death from a purely earthly perspective ("We look'd on this side of thee, shooting short") and for that reason saw only decaying bodies, themselves unable to cry, yet making *us* (the grieving ones left behind) do so. But Christ's death has beautified pale, bony, dusty death, giving it good color! Now we see it fair and full of grace. It's even desirable. Why? Christ's death recenters our sight. We see death as a door, for Christ's death finished death's finality. On its far side are blessed and beautified saints. So, Herbert says, we may just as well die as sleep, we may just as well use pillows of dust as of down, because we know we'll rise from death as surely as from slumber. In hope, we may commit our bodies ("Half that we have") to the grave. Notice Herbert's theological acumen and poetic power in the first and last words of the poem ("death" and "dust"). God told Adam, "for you are dust, and to dust you shall return" (Gen. 3:19). Ever since, dust is linked with human frailty and mortality. But see how Herbert fills it with new meaning, making it a pillow on which we rest until resurrection. Herbert's transformation of "dust" is, of course, a miniature version of the poem's larger message. Christ's death changes everything.

Shepherded by the poem. Look carefully at the shape of this poem. Do you see the shrinking and swelling of each stanza? Death diminishes us. It's our enemy. It takes health, friendship, life itself. Funerals are sad (and should be). But for followers of Christ, defeated death is now our path to resurrection bodies, perfect fellowship, eternal joy with God. Do you fear death? Allow Herbert to ground your hope and guide you toward your Christ-bought freedom.

Love (3)

Love bade me welcome: yet my soul drew back,
                    Guilty of dust and sin.
But quick-ey'd Love, observing me grow slack
                    From my first entrance in,
Drew nearer to me, sweetly questioning,
                    If I lack'd any thing.

A guest, I answer'd, worthy to be here:
                    Love said, You shall be he.
I the unkind, ungrateful? Ah my dear,
                    I cannot look on thee.
Love took my hand, and smiling did reply,
                    Who made the eyes but I?

Truth Lord, but I have marr'd them: let my shame
                    Go where it doth deserve.
And know you not, says Love, who bore the blame?
                    My dear, then I will serve.
You must sit down, says Love, and taste my meat:
                    So I did sit and eat.

Slack: sluggish.

Savoring the poem. This final, famous poem of "The Church" section has been described as "one of the greatest poems in the English language."[32] Quite right. Like all Herbert's best work, it's laden with meaning, yet light on its feet. It doesn't crush you with heavy truth, like a piano dropped from the fifth floor. Instead, its music moves you to discover more of the God who helps and holds. Here is a poem that (like Mary Poppins's carpet bag) is bigger on the inside than the outside. It's just eighteen lines. It uses the everyday imagery of hospitality and narrates a rather ordinary back-and-forth-conversation between an eager host and a reticent guest. But look closer and you'll notice numerous allusions to biblical passages (e.g. Matt. 22:1–10; Luke 12:37: 1 John 4:8; Rev. 19:9). Closer still, and you'll see all redemptive history, from the fall ("dust and sin") to redemption ("who bore the blame") and new creation ("So I did sit and eat"). Even closer, and now you'll experience for yourself the vast, eager, "quick-ey'd" love of God. Will you let sweet Love answer all your guilty objections, gainsay all your prideful attempts to serve and instead, seat and serve *you?* Will you savor the bread and cup of Communion, enjoying a foretaste of the new creation? The table is spread. Love smiles. Sit and eat!

Shepherded by the poem. What prevents you from fully receiving God's love? Guilt? Shame? Pride? How long have you been holding yourself apart from God? Feel his quick eye upon you. He's more eager to receive you than you are to respond. He always has more to give than we have the capacity to accept. Embrace his grace afresh for yourself. Allow him to serve you and draw you near with his love.

Conclusion

I HAVE EXCELLENT NEWS for all who love the poems you've experienced in this book: there's much more Herbert to explore and enjoy. There are poems you haven't yet read that will grow inside you, altering your understanding of God and his world. There are lines and phrases that will go deep and linger long. Here's a small sample of some I treasure but couldn't include in this volume:

- "Praise thee brimful!" (from "Dullness").
- "For where thou only wert before an executioner at best; Thou art a gard'ner now, and more . . ." (from "Time").
- "But such a heart, whose pulse may be Thy praise" (from "Gratefulness").
- "Lord, mend or rather make us . . ." (from "Giddiness")
- "Their hands convey him, who conveys their hands" (from "The Priesthood").
- "He is thy night at noon: he is at night Thy noon alone" (from "The Discharge").

We've only dipped our toes into the work of this remarkable pastor-poet. Three quarters of *The Temple* lies before you. The pool is open and the water's fine. Jump on in.

For further exploration, you'll want to have an edition of the complete English poems. Which edition(s) you use will depend on how deep you want to dive. My favorite three volumes (in order from popular to scholarly) are:

- John Drury and Victoria Moul, eds., *George Herbert: The Complete Poetry* (Penguin Random House UK, 2015). Drury is a lauded Herbert scholar. His brief comments on the poems are invariably accessible, incisive, and interesting.
- Ann Pasternak Slater, ed., *The Complete English Works of George Herbert* (Everyman's Library, 1995). This volume includes a helpful introduction, commentary on the poems, *The Country Parson*, other Herbert writings, and Izaak Walton's early biography (which is fascinating, but must be read with care since Walton is often hagiographic and historically unreliable).
- Helen Wilcox, ed., *The English Poems of George Herbert* (Cambridge University Press, 2007). This important volume provides an overview of major scholarship on all Herbert's English poems. It's essential for those seeking scholarly interaction and insight.

Another way to better understand Herbert's poetry is to learn more about his life. John Drury's biography, *Music at Midnight: The Life and Poetry of George Herbert* (Penguin Random House UK, 2014), compellingly interprets the life and poetry together. It's a fascinating account of a man with a rather uneventful external life but a richly complex interior one.

Other helpful resources include volumes of selected Herbert poems (with commentary) by Jim Scott Orrick, *A Year with George Herbert* (Wipf & Stock, 2011) and Mark Oakley, *My Sour-Sweet Days: George*

Herbert and the Journey of the Soul (SPCK, 2019). T. S. Eliot's slender volume *George Herbert* (Northcote, 1994) is rich with insight, as is Helen Vendler's *The Poetry of George Herbert* (Harvard University Press, 1975), Gene Edward Veith's *Reformation Spirituality: The Religion of George Herbert* (Wipf & Stock, 2013),[33] and Joseph Summers's *George Herbert: His Religion and Art* (Chatto and Windus, 1954).

But please don't just read books about Herbert. Read Herbert himself. Live with him. Carry the poems you especially love with you and allow them to stir your affections, inform your thought, and shape your life. I've read and wrestled with Herbert's poetry in the woods of New Hampshire, the Antrim coast of Northern Ireland, and the garden of Gethsemane. "Aaron" has ministered to me on countless early Sunday mornings when I've awakened despairing of my ability to serve God's people. I've often prayed the words of the Anglican liturgy for Herbert's feast day (words that are based on Herbert's "The Elixir"). During one particularly spiritually rich month, I read "Prayer (1)," focusing each day on one of its twenty-seven descriptions of prayer. I was marvelously guided by Malcolm Guite's cycle of twenty-seven sonnets (each engaging with one of Herbert's descriptions of prayer) published in *After Prayer: New Sonnets and Other Poems* (Canterbury Press, 2019).

Most important of all, as you read these poems, don't let your gaze terminate on the poet. Instead, see heaven through Herbert.

Teach me, my God and King,
    In all things thee to see.

. . .

A man that looks on glass,
    On it may stay his eye;

Or if he pleaseth, through it pass,
  And then the heav'n espy.

"The Elixir"

Herbert looked through everything and saw his God and King. And we can look through Herbert and see the glorious Christ he saw and served. I pray that, as you engage with Herbert, you'll come to enjoy more of Christ himself, and that your heart will be muttering all the day, *My joy, my life, my crown.*

Acknowledgments

IT'S A PLEASURE to acknowledge the many friends who have had a hand in forming this book.

Thanks to John and Alysia Yates, who gave me *The Complete Works of George Herbert* for my twenty-eighth birthday. Though I took quite a while to get to it, it's borne good fruit!

Thanks to Anthony Cirilla for his excellent Davenant Institute course on "George Herbert's Pastoral Poetics."

Thanks to those who read and commented on early ideas, early drafts, and later versions, including John Koontz, Andrew Witmer, Laura Sterrett, the fellows of the Center for Pastor Theologians, the editorial team at Desiring God, the leadership team of Small Town Summits, and the Gospel Guys.

Thanks to Randy and Jill Thompson, for graciously hosting me at Forest Haven for a rich week of writing in the woods of New Hampshire.

Thanks to Todd Augustine, Doug O'Donnell, Samuel James, and Laura Yiesla of Crossway, for encouraging me and improving this book.

My wife Emma and our children Samuel, Annie, and Henry are my favorite people in the world. I thank God for the joy of sharing life with them.

I've dedicated this volume to the people of Pepperell Christian Fellowship, whom I've served as a pastor for more than seventeen years. Thank you for your partnership in the gospel and for your generosity and kingdom vision in allowing me to write. Thank you for embracing all my sermon references to George Herbert! You're dear to me. You're "all my joy and thought" (in Herbert's words). Serving and shepherding you is a tremendous privilege.

Notes

1. Portions of this introduction first appeared in Stephen Witmer, "The Temple: A Reader's Guide to a Christian Classic," *Desiring God,* March 21, 2023.
2. David Werther and Susan Werther, eds., *C. S. Lewis's List: The Ten Books That Influenced Him Most* (Bloomsbury, 2015), 2.
3. Miranda Threlfall-Holmes, "George Herbert: The Man Who Converted Me from Atheism," *The Guardian,* February 17, 2014, https://www.theguardian.com/us.
4. Dennis O'Driscoll, *Stepping Stones: Interviews with Seamus Heaney* (Faber and Faber, 2008), 50.
5. The text of all forty poems in this volume is from the "The Temple," Christian Classics Ethereal Library (CCEL) website, accessed May 23, 2025, https://www.ccel.org/h/herbert/temple/PoemTOC.html, which uses the 1633 edition of *The Temple.* The poems selected here follow the same order of that edition as well. The language has been lightly modernized and British spellings Americanized.
6. T. S. Eliot, *George Herbert* (Northcote, 1994), 28–29.
7. Robert Frost, quoted in Abram Van Engen, *Word Made Fresh: An Invitation to Poetry for the Church* (Eerdmans, 2024), 89.
8. Van Engen, *Word Made Fresh,* 42.
9. Helen Wilcox, "'Hallow'd Fire'; or, When Is a Poet Not a Priest?" in *George Herbert's Pastoral: New Essays on the Poet and Priest of Bemerton,* ed. Christopher Hodgkins (University of Delaware Press, 2010), 101.
10. Helen Wilcox, ed., *The English Poems of George Herbert* (Cambridge University Press, 2007), xxi.

11. Gene Edward Veith, *Reformation Spirituality: The Religion of George Herbert* (1985; repr., Wipf & Stock, 2013), 247, describes Herbert as a Calvinist "whose theology, and thus poetry, is radically 'God-centered.'"
12. Veith, *Reformation Spirituality*, 250.
13. John Drury, *Music at Midnight: The Life and Poetry of George Herbert* (Penguin Random House UK, 2014), 252.
14. Timothy Keller, *The Meaning of Marriage* (Dutton, 2011), 48.
15. John Drury and Victoria Moul, eds., *George Herbert: The Complete Poetry* (Penguin Random House UK, 2015), 387.
16. Wilcox, *English Poems of George Herbert*,165.
17. Wilcox, *English Poems of George Herbert*, 180–81.
18. Drury and Moul, *George Herbert*, 404.
19. Richard Strier, *Love Known: Theology and Experience in George Herbert's Poetry* (Chicago: University of Chicago Press, 1983), 89.
20. Strier, *Love Known*, 91.
21. Joseph Summers, *George Herbert: His Religion and Art* (Chatto and Windus, 1954), 153.
22. Ann Pasternak Slater, ed., *The Complete English Works of George Herbert* (Everyman's Library, 1995), 446.
23. Wilcox, *English Poems of George Herbert*, 499.
24. Slater, *Herbert*, 463.
25. Drury and Moul, *George Herbert*, 455.
26. Wilcox, *English Poems of George Herbert*, 528.
27. Augustine, *The Confessions* (Alfred A. Knopf, 2001), 5.
28. C. S. Lewis, *Mere Christianity* (Simon & Schuster, 1996), 121.
29. Drury and Moul, *George Herbert*, 469.
30. Barnabas Oley, quoted in Drury and Moul, *George Herbert*, 471.
31. Oxford English Dictionary, under "Cordials," accessed June 6, 2025, https://www.oed.com/?tl=true.
32. Drury and Moul, *George Herbert*, 485.
33. This is a reprint of Veith's *Reformation Spirituality* (Associated University Presses, 1985).

Person Index

Scripture Index